Adopted:
The Preciousness of the Family of God

By Matthew Allen

© 2024 Spiritbuilding Publishers.
All rights reserved. No part of this book may be reproduced in any form without the written permission of the publisher.

Published by
Spiritbuilding Publishers
9700 Ferry Road, Waynesville, Ohio 45068

ADOPTED
The Preciousness of the Family of God
By Matthew Allen

ISBN: 978-1964805-02-3

Unless otherwise noted, all Scripture references are taken from Holman Bible Publishers' Christian Standard Bible.

Spiritbuilding
PUBLISHERS

spiritbuilding.com

Table of Contents

Introduction 1

Lesson 1   A New Identity 5

Lesson 2   New Family Values 14

Lesson 3   Spiritual Family 23

Lesson 4   Gifted, Godly Leaders 29

Lesson 5   Freedom from Sin 36

Lesson 6   A Peace Not Like the World 44

Lesson 7   A Different Outlook on Life 53

Lesson 8   A Different Outlook on Death 62

Lesson 9   Spiritual Confidence 71

Lesson 10   The Experience and Wonder of Worship 82

Lesson 11   The Excitement of Sharing Our Hope 93

Lesson 12   A Wealth of Spiritual Blessings 100

Introduction

Sons and Daughters of God

2013, my 39th year, was a year of extreme change. My parents, who had spent the previous twelve years in South Dakota, planned to move back east to Ohio to be near me and my family. My dad had fallen into poor health, and my mom needed help. In January of that year, I traveled out to help them pack up. It was an emotional trip. Our family had fallen in love with South Dakota, the church family there, and the beautiful scenery of the Black Hills. Over the years, I have discovered that people either love it or hate it there … and if you are one of the ones who fall in love with the Black Hills, it is tough to let go. That was certainly the case for us. I remember helping Mom and Dad go through their things—and one day, we came across a document that held a significance far beyond its legal terminology—a faded adoption certificate. As I traced the worn edges, a flood of emotions enveloped me, transporting me back to my childhood, where I had been welcomed into the warm embrace of a family I now call my own. It was a day that signified the legal affirmation of my belonging and the unconditional love that had enveloped me from the beginning of my relationship with the man who would be my father.

This document, a piece of paper to some, symbolizes my adoption journey. It has shaped my understanding of love and family and mirrored the spiritual adoption we experience as Christians into God's diverse and everlasting family. It has taught me the true essence of grace, acceptance, and the boundless love of a family chosen not by blood but by heart.

As I write these thoughts, I feel a deep sense of gratitude and reflection. My story is but one in the untold numbers of adoption stories that span cultures, histories, and religions yet find common ground in the universal language of love. Through sharing my experience, I want to peel back the layers of what it means to be adopted—into a loving home on earth and the eternal embrace of our heavenly Father. It's a personal exploration of how being chosen and loved without precondition is similar to the most incredible story ever told in the scriptures. It offers us a glimpse into the heart of God Himself—a heart that adopts, loves, and redeems.

I want you to discover this study's beautiful, complex, redemptive adoption story. It's a story of finding a home, being chosen, and ultimately, belonging to a family far more significant than we could ever imagine.

Adoption is a powerful word. It describes a concept filled with love, mercy, and grace. When an adoption happens, a person is taken into a family not related to them and given all the rights and privileges of a family member. If you've experienced adoption in your physical family, you know it is just something truly incredible. I know this from personal experience. Fifty years ago, on May 5, 1974, my biological father was killed in a hunting accident directly in front of my mother. They had only been married for around 16 months. The emotional trauma of that day still affects her. I do not remember my father; I was only a little over nine weeks old. After that, my mother moved back in with her parents. It was a very dark time for my family. Mom met Sam Allen two years later, whom she would later marry. Sam (dad) adopted me. Ever since I've been welcomed as if I were a flesh and blood member of the Allen family, it's been such a blessing. In 2013, as we were preparing to move my parents back east, we came across the adoption document signed by a judge in 1980. I love the language of the last paragraph of the judge's writing:

> IT IS THEREFORE BY THE COURT CONSIDERED AND ORDERED, that Joseph Matthew Tyler Harvey Allen be and he is hereby permanently adopted to the Petitioners, Sam Allen and Donna Allen, his natural mother, for all intents and purposes as though he had been the natural child of both; that the Bureau of Vital Statistics of the State Health Department of Arkansas should be and hereby is authorized and directed to substitute the child's birth certificate showing the Petitioners as his parents. IT IS SO ORDERED.

I have been very blessed by the graciousness of my father, Sam Allen, who brought me into his family. I will be forever thankful for God's direction in getting him into my life. I was blessed to have him for 37 brief years of my life, as he died a few days before Christmas in 2013. His great patience with me, love, and leadership helped make me who I am today.

There are many stories of adoption in the Bible. At least three instances occur in the Old Testament. Moses (Exodus 2) and Esther (Esther 2) are examples. But, perhaps the most compelling adoption story is in 2 Samuel

9 with David's adoption of Saul's grandson, Mephibosheth. Saul had been the continual enemy of David, doing everything he could to kill him. Saul's jealousy, hatred, and pride are almost unrivaled. Saul's character stands in great contrast to his son Jonathan, who was David's closest friend and confidant. At the age of five, Mephibosheth was paralyzed when his caretaker dropped him, 2 Samuel 4:4. After David came to power, what was left of Saul's family fell out of the spotlight.

David took the initiative and extended kindness to Jonathan's sons. They searched the kingdom and found Mephibosheth, who dwelled in Lo-debar, or "the barren land." There was nothing worse in society than to be crippled. Mephibosheth offered nothing to society. Even the meaning of his name ("A Shameful Thing") indicated his low place in the world. He was from the family of an enemy. When David moved to adopt Mephibosheth, it was an act of grace (2 Samuel 9:6–7). Because of David's kindness and love, which Mephibosheth did nothing to earn, he could enter the palace *as one of the king's sons* (9:11b). In a culture that ostracized the crippled and lame, Mephibosheth ate at the king's table! How amazing is that?

Other than God's demonstration of grace and mercy to sinners, there is perhaps no better story in the Bible related to adoption than this. David's adoption of Mephibosheth is how God adopts us today. God took the initiative by sending His son and showed mercy to those unworthy, Romans 5:6. God moves to save us with His incredible love and kindness (Ephesians 2:6–7). God redeemed us when we were far beyond perfection and gave us an inheritance (1 Peter 1:3–4). This adoption is for all who will separate themselves unto the Lord and *cleanse themselves* (2 Corinthians 6:17—7:1).

In Romans 8, Paul moved to establish how Christians have assurance in their salvation. We stand in and live by grace. We've been adopted into the family of God. Notice how Paul writes Romans 8:14–16, where he says all who the Spirit of God leads are **sons of God:**

> For you did not receive the spirit of slavery to fall back into fear, but you have received the Spirit of **adoption as sons**, by whom we cry, "Abba! Father!" The Spirit himself bears witness with our spirit that we are **children of God** [emphasis mine].

These terms are significant and should help quell our fears about our status as sons and daughters of God.

Consider ancient kings "adopting" a successor or declaring, when passing the rule to his son, "This is my own son." This gives us a greater understanding of what it means to be sons and daughters of God!

The idea of adoption and sonship extends to joint rule with Christ. This is seen in Paul's thoughts in Ephesians 1:15—2:10. The *Father of Glory* raised Jesus and seated Him at His right hand. We have been made alive (2:5), raised by the power that raised Jesus, and seated with Christ (2:6). This is *the immeasurable greatness of his power toward us who believe, according to the working of his great might, that he worked in Christ when he raised him from the dead,* (1:19–20). Christ is seated at the right hand of God. We are seated with Christ. We are enthroned with Him. We are restored to the rule for which we were created! See Genesis 1:26, 28.

Through the lens of physical and spiritual adoption, we are reminded that our origins and circumstances do not determine our worth or the flaws we carry but by the love that chooses us, embraces us, and calls us by name into a new family.

The stories of Moses, Esther, Mephibosheth, and countless others throughout history who have found a home in the hearts of those not bound to them by blood mirror our spiritual adoption into God's family. This act of grace, where we are welcomed with open arms regardless of our past or burdens, offers an unforgettable insight into the heart of belonging, being loved, and being part of something greater than ourselves.

As we reflect on the significance of adoption, let us embrace our identity as beloved children of God and live out that reality in how we treat others. Spiritual adoption, filled with its trials and triumphs, ultimately points us toward the fact that there is always room for one more at the table in God's family. May we carry forward the legacy of love and acceptance we have received that touch the lives of those around us, reminding us that we are indeed chosen, cherished, and adopted into an eternal family?

Lesson 1

A New Identity

Living as God's Masterpiece:
The Art of Grace-Filled Living

Before You Begin

Read Ephesians 2:1–10.

Pray for insight, asking God for understanding, wisdom, and the ability to see how these things apply to your life.

Introduction

In this lesson, we will discuss the concept of salvation and how it is often brought to light by the beautiful metaphor of adoption. Ephesians 2 and Paul's teachings clarify this, describing our journey from spiritual desolation to divine belonging. By exploring God's initiative, the reason behind our salvation, and its results, we can see a parallel to the adoption process, where one is chosen, redeemed, and given a new identity.

How did God make our salvation happen? The first ten verses of Ephesians 2 detail how God brought it all about. Here, Paul tells us how God moved with swift urgency to save us from spiritual disaster and His wrath. He also goes into detail about the depths of our desperate situation. Here we learn:

- How *God took* the initiative to save.
- Why *God decided* to save.
- The result of the salvation *God provides*.

There are some fantastic contrasts presented here:

Powerful Contrasts in Ephesians 2:1–7

Your Past Life	Your New Life
Dead in Sin (2:1)	Alive in Christ (2:5–6)
Enslaved to the Spirit of the Age (2:2)	Freed to Sit with Christ in Heaven (2:6)
Children of Wrath (2:3)	Recipient of Endless Kindness (2:7)

All these things are amazing, incomprehensible, and incredibly awesome! We are recipients of His power, care, compassion, and love. And to think, this is all about God's plan and activity. You breathe today because of His magnificent love and abundant and rich grace. We must hold on to these facts and keep them in our minds.

In the following pages, we want to focus on our new identity in Christ. But before we do, embracing the present reality of your salvation is crucial.

Your Salvation: A Present Reality

We too all previously lived among them in our fleshly desires, carrying out the inclinations of our flesh and thoughts, and we were by nature children under wrath as the others were also.

But God, who is rich in mercy, because of his great love that he had for us,

The contrast between Ephesians 2:3 and 2:4 cannot be more significant. In these verses, we observe two groups of people: children under wrath and a different set of children who have been shown mercy. Inherent in all of this is our choice. We may choose to be either God's enemies or His children. Those who choose God receive mercy, which removes deserved punishment.

John writes:

> God's love was revealed among us in this way: God sent his one and only Son into the world so that we might live through him. Love consists in this: not that we loved God, but that he loved us and sent his Son to be the atoning sacrifice for our sins (1 John 4.9–10).

God took the initiative by demonstrating pity and compassion toward us after we fell into a situation that we could not escape without help. The fact that we became victims because of our bad choices did not prevent God from having mercy. God loves us no matter what.

In Ephesians 1, Paul spoke about the *power* available to *us who believe* (1:19–20). By His power, God raised Jesus from the dead. By that same power, God raises us from spiritual death (2:5). *God brings dead people to life.* God seated Jesus at His right hand in the heavenly places by His *power* (1:20b). By that same power, God has *seated us with him in the heavenly places in Christ*

Jesus (2:5b). Just as Jesus lives forever and reigns triumphantly, so do God's children continue in spiritual life and triumph over the old life of human failure. *What you were, you are no longer, by the grace of God.*

In Ephesians 2:5, *saved* is written in the present tense. Salvation by grace is not just a future promise but a present reality. Notice how Paul goes on to describe that reality:

- You are alive *together* with Christ.
- You have been raised *together* with Christ.
- You are seated *together* with Christ.

A Parallel Text

> giving thanks to the Father, who has enabled you to share in the saints' inheritance in the light. He has rescued us from the domain of darkness and transferred us into the kingdom of the Son he loves (Colossians 1:12–13).

Please focus on the words *rescued* and *transfer*. These are powerful. *Rescued* means "to be delivered." This is God's ultimate goal in history.

Look at how Jesus summarized His mission:

> The Spirit of the Lord is on me, because he has anointed me to preach good news to the poor. He has sent me to proclaim release to the captives and recovery of sight to the blind, to set free the oppressed (Luke 4:18).

Transferred means "a change of state, emphasizing the difference in the resulting state." It is "a change in position," "a change of residence." You have been taken from Satan's domain and transferred to God's.

Now let's examine Colossians 2:12–14:

> When you were buried with him in baptism, in which you were also raised with him through faith in the working of God, who raised him from the dead. And when you were dead in trespasses and in the uncircumcision of your flesh, he made you alive with him and forgave us all our trespasses. He erased the certificate of debt, with its obligations, that was against us and opposed to us and has taken it away by nailing it to the cross.

You had piled up a debt before God. Its payment was death. Now, Jesus caused it all to be set aside. Your sins were nailed to His cross.

The Best News Ever

> For you are saved by grace through faith, not from yourselves; it is God's gift—not from works, so that no one can boast (Ephesians 2:8–9).

When Paul says, this is not from yourselves; he is teaching that salvation is a gift from God's abundant kindness and lavish grace. There is nothing within us that has inclined God to choose us. There will never be enough good deeds to warrant a favorable verdict from God on the day of judgment. God's way of salvation eliminates human boasting.

Your New Identity: A Masterpiece of Grace

In Ephesians 2:7, Paul wrote that God wants to demonstrate the immeasurable riches of His grace through Jesus for all eternity. True love and grace will always find a way to express themselves to the benefit of the one loved. We have a God who is eager to display His lovingkindness.

> He has not dealt with us as our sins deserve or repaid us according to our iniquities. For as high as the heavens are above the earth, so great is his faithful love toward those who fear him. As far as the east is from the west, so far has he removed our transgressions from us. As a father has compassion on his children, so the Lord has compassion on those who fear him. For he knows what we are made of, remembering that we are dust (Psalm 103:10–14).

Malachi said that we are God's treasured possession. We will always be His treasured possession—now and forever more.

God's Workmanship

Let's look at verse 10. "For" connects to the verb in 2:8a. Paul is building on his point that salvation has nothing to do with human effort. Here, Paul uses two words to speak of this new creation: *workmanship* and *created*. "Workmanship" emphasizes the *craftsmanship* or *design* of the creator, such as the potter's skill in producing a jar … or the literary skill of a writer in composing poetry. See how some of the other translations handle this word:

- NIV: we are God's handiwork.
- NLT: For we are God's masterpiece.
- NAB: handiwork.
- NJB: work of art.

It is not that "we will be" God's workmanship. But "we are" God's workmanship. It is written in the *present tense,* meaning right now. You are God's work of art –even with all your imperfections and room to grow. Who are you in Christ? You are a living display of grace. You are someone special. You are valuable. You are important. You mean something. God loves you.

God's Creation

"Created" is the more common word for God's act of creation. The exact wording is found in 2 Corinthians 5:17:

> Therefore, if anyone is in Christ, he is a new creation; the old has passed away, and see, the new has come!

Paul uses it in Ephesians 4:24. He says you are a new person who has been created in God's likeness in true righteousness and holiness.

Why Did God Recreate You?

Why have you been recreated in Christ Jesus? *For good **works**.* You display God's grace by doing good works. Your works are NEVER about you. They're all about God and who He is. Paul stresses that the new order of our lives produces good works. Here, works are not performed to secure salvation but as the fruit of salvation. Good works are the *fruit,* not the *root,* of the tree of salvation.

Jesus said:

> I am the vine; you are the branches. The one who remains in me and I in him produces much fruit because you can do nothing without me, John 15:5.

Those in Christ will bear much fruit, not as a requirement for admission, but because of their union with him. If there are no good works in your life, it is evidence or symptom of a fundamental problem: a lack of a vital relationship with Christ. If you're lost after having once been saved, it's not going to be because you didn't work enough … it's going to be because you didn't know Jesus as you should. The more you understand the Father, the more you'll imitate Him.

Embrace Your New Status

As we go through the ups and downs of living in the flesh, it is prevalent for Christians to fight fierce battles with the flesh. After we sin, we must refuse to dwell in disappointment. When we do, it is essential to remember our righteousness.

- You have been made new (2 Corinthians 5:17). Now, you walk in newness of life (Romans 6:4).
- You have eternal life (Titus 3:7).
- You have become fit for the presence of God (Ephesians 2:19).
- You have *purified* your *soul by* obeying *the truth* (1 Peter 1:22). Remember that you have obeyed the gospel. You have believed, repented, and been baptized. In 1:22, *purified* is in the present perfect tense, indicating past action with continuing results.
- You have been washed, purified, and given new life. When you were baptized, you put on the new man (Ephesians 4:24).
- You have been recreated for righteousness and holiness. This birth is not by *perishable seed*, but *imperishable* (1 Peter 1:22–23).
- You are now a *partaker of the divine nature* (2 Peter 1:4). God has given you a new identity.

We must never steal God's glory by discounting what He has made us. Rather than living in constant disappointment, we must live the way Paul does in Romans 7. Upon examining ourselves, we will find we do things we do not want. We will do things that are inconsistent with who we are. As we do, we need to see that sin as an intrusion into who we are in Christ. We must hate the sin we see, confess it to God, and treat it, at best, as an unwelcome guest or, at worst, as an invasion by a fierce and threatening enemy.

But that is no longer who you are. Sin no longer defines who you are. You have been redeemed as Christ's possession. You *want to do what is good.* You *do not want to do what is evil.* You want to serve the law of God. This is who you are in Christ. Paul looked forward to the day he would be delivered from his body of sin and death, Romans 7:24. Death will involve separation from the physical body. You will be liberated from the flesh and set free to be everything you were created to be when you were made new in Christ.

What's In This for Us?

Embrace your new identity in Christ daily. Just as an adopted child grows into their new family identity, we have been called to embrace our identity as children of God daily. Begin each day with a prayer, thanking God for His mercy and grace and asking for His guidance to live out your identity in Christ. Affirmations based on scripture can reinforce your sense of belonging and purpose, reminding you that you are loved, chosen, and redeemed.

Live out the reality of your spiritual adoption through acts of kindness. Your adoption into God's family is marked by love and grace. You have been called to reflect these in your dealings with others. Look for opportunities to extend kindness and compassion to those around you, demonstrating the mercy you've received. This could be as simple as lending a listening ear, offering support to someone in need, or volunteering your time and resources to help others. Acts of kindness are practical expressions of God's love through us.

Build your belonging within the body of Christ. Being adopted into God's family means you are part of His church. Actively participate in your local congregation to cultivate a sense of belonging and connection. Engage in small group studies, join service projects, or try to build relationships with fellow believers. Encouraging, serving, and bearing one another's burdens are practical ways to live out your spiritual adoption and strengthen the body of Christ.

Reflect on your journey and share your story. Just as an adopted child might reflect on their journey to becoming part of their family, reflect on your spiritual life. Journaling can be a powerful tool, helping you see how God has worked in your life. Sharing your story with others can be an encouragement to them and a testimony to God's grace. It's a reminder that God is still active and working, drawing people to Himself and transforming lives.

Extend the invitation of spiritual adoption to others. As someone who has experienced the power of being adopted into God's family, you can share this gift with others. Engage in conversations about your faith, offer to pray for and with those exploring Christianity, and be ready to communicate the reason for your hope. Invite friends to church services or events to learn more about God's love and the beauty of a relationship with God. Being a bridge for others to find their way into God's family is one of the most profound ways to live out the grace you've been given.

Conclusion

Our journey of spiritual adoption redefines our relationship with God and reshapes our understanding of ourselves. We are no longer defined by our past or sins but by our new status in Christ—as part of God's family, destined for good works and bearers of His image. Embracing this truth empowers us to live out our days in confidence, not in the shadow of our former selves but in the light of God's redeeming love.

We must remember and live out our adopted status. Just as adoption changes a child's life trajectory, being adopted into Christ has altered our eternal destiny. We are invited to leave behind the old domains of sin and death and step into the light of God's kingdom, walking in the newfound identity and purpose He has graciously given us. Through this understanding, we can genuinely appreciate the depths of God's love and the power of spiritual adoption.

For Reflection

1. How does adoption in human families mirror our spiritual adoption into God's family?

2. What does being a 'child of God' mean to you personally, and how does it influence your daily life and decisions?

3. How does understanding your identity as God's adopted child impact your view of yourself and others around you?

4. In what ways have you experienced the transformative power of God's grace and mercy in your life? Can you share a specific instance where you felt truly embraced by God's love?

5. Ephesians 2 speaks of moving from death to life through Christ's mercy and power. How does this transition manifest in the lives of Christians today?

6. Considering the act of choosing involved in adoption, what does it mean to you that God chose you to be a part of His family?

7. How can the church better represent the inclusive, adopting love of God to those outside the four walls of its building?

8. Discuss the challenge of living out our new identity in Christ amid a world that often does not understand or accept it. How do you navigate this tension?

9. Reflect on the concept of 'good works' being the fruit of our salvation, not the root. How can believers demonstrate these fruits in their community and daily interactions?

10. Spiritual adoption brings with it a new inheritance and promises from God. How do these promises shape the hope and perspective of believers, especially during difficult times?

Lesson 2

New Family Values

Reshaping Your Identity from the Inside Out

Before You Begin

Read Ephesians 4:17–32.

Pray for God to help you continue your pursuit of transformation, embracing His spiritual values more and more every day.

Introduction

Going through the adoption process marks a deeply personal and significant shift in an individual's life. When a person is adopted, it involves a transition from one family to another. This change goes beyond legalities and paperwork; it's about leaving behind old family values, traditions, and identities to embrace new ones fully. As an adopted child becomes part of their new family, they take on its values, beliefs, and ways of life, which fundamentally shape their understanding of the world and their place within it. This change represents a new beginning, filled with love and belonging, a newfound identity.

Similarly, the New Testament speaks of a spiritual adoption that parallels physical adoption but dives deeper into the soul. By faith, believers are adopted into God's family, becoming His children with all the benefits and responsibilities that come with it. This spiritual adoption profoundly shifts our identity, values, and allegiances. Reborn in spirit, Christians leave their former selves behind to embrace God's values, beliefs, and mission (2 Corinthians 5:17).

Adoption reshapes our identity from the inside out. Our relationship with God, rooted in this newfound identity, becomes the core of our existence. When we come to Christ, God pulls us out of the shadows and brings us into His divine family. Old ways of thinking, fears, and doubts are in the past. In their place, we embrace a new set of values—love, forgiveness, and hope. We see God as a loving Father, guiding, protecting, and nurturing us toward a purposeful life. When God brings us into His family, He transforms us, shaping us into someone who seeks to spread love and kindness in every way possible.

Your story as a Christian is a living testimony to what it means to be chosen and loved. It's about finding where you truly belong and discovering the incredible life that unfolds when you come to Christ. Being spiritually adopted by God is incredibly personal and impacts how you view yourself, your purpose in life, and your relationship with God and those around you. As we further explore this concept, we'll examine the deep spiritual, emotional, and ethical dimensions of what it truly means to be chosen and adopted by God and how this new life He offers us reshapes everything.

A great passage in our Bibles reflects the type of change for the one who has been adopted into Christ. Ephesians 4:17–32 presents us with an efficient picture of mature Christian living. It could be argued that Paul's line of thought here continues from where he left off in 4:3 as he describes the daily walk with Christ.

What does it mean to live a worthy life? What is the new standard of conduct called for here?

Ephesians 4:17–21: Don't Live Like You Used To

We must remove ourselves from our former lifestyle when we come to Christ. *You should no longer walk as the Gentiles do* (4:17). To unity and maturity, purity must be applied. As you read here, remember that the thought is carried forth into verses 22–24. Paul is developing his argument of a complete separation between the old and new lives through Christ. There can be no mixing of the two (Matthew 6:24; Luke 9:62). We must be totally committed to moving toward maturity.

This Begins with Our Thinking

As you read 4:17b, notice where Paul begins. In the *futility of their thoughts*. See how he doesn't start with action. He begins with the mind. Here, he describes the emptiness of those who do not know God. The word implies "vanity, foolishness, and frustration." Faulty thinking led the Gentiles to have their moral distinctions blurred. As we reflect on Paul's writing earlier in

Ephesians, notice how he speaks about their hearts being enlightened by the Spirit.

> I pray that the God of our Lord Jesus Christ, the glorious Father, would give you the Spirit of wisdom and revelation in the knowledge of him (Ephesians 1:17).

Those in the world had not been enlightened. They did not know God or His ways.

Ultimately, this thinking led to their separation from God because of their ignorance and hardness of heart (4:18). *Ignorance* here should be understood as "the refusal to know." It is not an excuse; it is a willful sin. You might compare it to Romans 1:18 and 25, where Paul said the Gentiles suppressed the truth by their wickedness and did not think it worthwhile to retain the knowledge of God. This ignorance is the product of a hard heart. *Hardening* was often used for a soft mass or tissue that had calcified or turned to stone.

Notice 4:19. What does the hardening process lead to?

- **Callousness**. The NIV refers to the loss of sensitivity. The idea is that a person can move beyond the point of feeling or care. See also 1 Timothy 4:2. Some had their consciences seared like an iron. The Gentiles reached a point where they no longer cared about the immorality that characterized their life.
- **Promiscuity**. This word is the strongest in Greek, denoting depravity, "indicating a total disregard for decency. It encompasses riotous and excessive living, frequently with unrestrained sexual behavior in view."
- **Impurity**. This is a work of the flesh (Galatians 5:19). It is summarized as "moral pollution."
- A **desire** to practice more and more. They coveted new ways to sin. Every different kind of sin was a new delicacy. They had an insatiable appetite for sin.

The Contrast

What is described in 4:17–19 directly contrasts with the Christian. As we study 4:20–24, these verses are more of a statement of fact than commands, although both are intertwined. Their lives had been made new by the work of Jesus on the cross. However, there was still the expectation to continue to put away the old thinking/actions and embrace the new.

In 4:20, Paul teaches that worldly thinking is not taught in Christ. Instead, we are made new in Christ. The mind and body are inseparably connected. We must change our thoughts to eliminate our old behavior. We must conform those thoughts to the truth in Jesus, 4:21. Jesus said, *you shall know the truth, and the truth will set you free* (John 8:32).

4:22–24—Three Essential Directives

What is essential to living inside the new reality created for us?

We are to:

- Put off our old self.
- Be renewed in the spirit of our mind.
- Put on the new self.

This makes up what could be called a *purpose statement for the new life*. You have been created after the likeness of God in true righteousness and holiness. Are you living inside this new reality?

Put Off the Old Self

The old self is the person who lived with sinful desires and was separated from God. Isaiah said:

> We have all become like one who is unclean, and all our righteous deeds are like a polluted garment. We all fade like a leaf, and our iniquities, like the wind, take us away (Isaiah 64:6).

Paul goes into specific detail in describing the old self in Ephesians 2:1–3:

> And you were dead in your trespasses and sins in which you previously walked according to the ways of this world, according to the ruler of the power of the air, the spirit now working in the disobedient. We too all previously lived among them in our fleshly desires, carrying out the inclinations of our flesh and thoughts, and we were by nature children under wrath as the others were also.

That person was put off in baptism, Romans 6:1–6. Your old self has been crucified. It is no more. You have been made new by the blood of Christ

(2 Corinthians 5:17; Colossians 2:11–15). This old person is no longer who you are.

But we still must deal with the flesh. It is corrupted by deceitful desires that lead to sin and error. If we choose not to resist, it will lead us to destruction.

Be Renewed in the Spirit of Your Mind

Remember what Paul said in 4:17b. He said the Gentiles walked *in the futility of their thoughts.* "Futility" describes the emptiness of those who do not know God. But now look again at 4:23. This presents the most remarkable contrast. Christians are being made new in the attitude of their minds. The renewal in 4:23 is continuous. It is not instantaneous but, instead, a process. It is the internal transformation Paul spoke of in Romans 12:2. Success against conformity to this world begins in your mind.

Put on the New Self

Remember Isaiah 64:6? This old person MUST be put off. Remember, you put on the new self in the water of baptism. You have been recreated in Christ. The phrase *put on* is unique to Paul's writing. He uses it in:

- Galatians 3:26–27 and Romans 13:14: *put on Christ.*
- Colossians 3:9–10: *put on the new self.*

The idea implies that we allow Jesus to rule in our lives. We live inside our new identity. This also involves present action. We must continue to resist the flesh. We must keep our righteous garments on and avoid the pitfalls that would lead us to stain them.

Why Did God Recreate You?

Did Paul have Genesis 1:26–27 in mind when he penned the words of Ephesians 4:24b? Notice that you have been created after the likeness of God in true righteousness and holiness. From the beginning, God has intended us to be righteous and holy before Him, 1:4. Paul's message is specific here. It urges our need to be consistent with what and who God is.

See the contrast between the *deceived* mind (4:22c) and the renewed mind (4:23). It's all about perspective. Consider yourselves dead to sin and alive to God (Romans 6:11). God has recreated you to be righteous and holy, as He is.

4:25–31—The New Reality

In 4:25–31, Paul discusses five things we can practice daily. These are visible demonstrations of what it means to live by our new family values.

Speak the Truth

In 4:25, Paul says that we need to stop speaking falsehoods. What sharper break could we make than abandoning this way of the world? Our world is full of lies and deceit. People lie all the time. Instead, we are to stand with God, who cannot lie (Hebrews 6:18). We can't tell half-truths. We must be able to share an honest, close association. Telling lies rips the fabric of unity in the one body. Always be willing to tell the truth.

Control Your Anger

In 4:26, Paul dealt with anger. This is a God-given emotion, but it must be held in check. Uncontrolled and sustained anger against a person is condemned in scripture. Jesus said *anyone angry with his brother will be subject to judgment* (Matthew 5:22). James said that man's *anger does not bring about the righteous life that God desires* (James 1:20).

Anger will come. But when it does, we must not sin. "An action taken in the heat of anger is almost always wrong." And, when it comes, it must be dealt with before the day ends. Few things are prioritized over seeking reconciliation with a brother (Matthew 5:24). Hatred must not be harbored as a growing resentment. This is why Paul said, give no opportunity to the devil (4:27). Satan will try to exploit the situation when emotions are out of control. Please don't give him room to operate.

Do Honest Work

In 4:28, Paul speaks about the value of work. The idea of productiveness and providing for oneself is seen throughout scripture. Those who stole (a continuing and habitual problem) were to stop stealing. Instead, they were to work hard for themselves and be on the lookout for others in need. Stealing is to be replaced by hard work—*the dignity of labor and the joy of sharing leave no room for the desire to steal.*

Speak for the Building Up

In 4:29, "Corrupting talk" is an interesting expression. "Corrupting" comes from a word associated with *rotten fruit, decayed trees,* and *spoiled fish.* Let that imagery sink into your mind for a moment. Jesus said that what comes out of our mouths defiles us because it reveals what is in our hearts (Matthew 15:11, 18). Corrupt words are those that do not build up.

Instead of speaking these kinds of words, we are to speak for the building up of others. If we can't say something positive, we should not talk. We need to realize the power of our words and direct them into something that will benefit others.

How have the words of someone else torn at your heart?

How have the words of encouragement from someone else built you up?

Why is this so important? Look at 4:30. We can grieve the Spirit by what we speak. See how personal this is. The Spirit speaks (1 Timothy 4:1), teaches (John 14:26), and intercedes (Romans 8:27). This passage teaches that the Spirit has feelings and can be grieved in a movingly personal way. See Isaiah 63:10.

Put Away Bitterness

In 4:31, Paul speaks of bitterness. This is "the temper which cherishes resentful feelings." It is a feeling of hatred and spite. It can lead to wrath and anger. Wrath usually describes the initial explosion of a hot temper. Anger is a "more settled feeling of gnawing hostility." If these things are unchecked, they can lead to clamor and slander. Clamor is shouting out in anger. It usually is governed by the mindset that the louder a person is, the stronger his point will be. Slander is the act of speaking against. It is "reviling and cursing," including "ominous and obscene words."

All of this is summed up in the word malice. This word refers to any attitude or action that intends to harm another person. This disposition has no place in the new person created in God's likeness.

Conclusion

Reflecting on adoption—both in its tangible and spiritual forms—is an enriching experience for the Christian. The path from a sinner to a beloved child of God defines our existence and identity at its very core. Spiritual adoption should become the most intimate chapter of our story. It shows us the purest form of love—that reaches into the shadows and places us in the center of grace, a love that transforms the essence of who we are. God's act of choosing us through the gospel, changing us, and welcoming us into His divine family is a deeply personal testament to His boundless grace and mercy.

Our spiritual adoption reshapes our hearts, renews our minds, and redefines our futures. Through the waters of baptism, we put off our old selves and step into a new reality, clothed in righteousness and holiness (Galatians 3:26–27). This new identity compels us to live out God's values daily, seeking to embody love, forgiveness, and hope in a world thirsty for truth.

As you embrace your place in God's family, never forget the incredible gift of belonging you have received. Let this knowledge fuel your purpose, guide your steps, and inspire you to spread the gracious love and kindness you have been given.

For Reflection

1. How does the concept or practice of adoption help us understand our relationship with God more deeply?

2. In what ways does spiritual adoption by God change our identity? How does this new identity affect our daily lives?

3. Reflecting on the transition from old family values to new ones in physical adoption, how does this compare to the spiritual renewing of our minds in Christ?

4. How does understanding our status as chosen and loved by God impact our sense of belonging and purpose?

5. Why is embracing our new values and identity in God's family necessary? Discuss the challenges that might prevent us from doing so.

6. How can the process of putting off the old self and putting on the new self, as mentioned in Ephesians 4:22–24, be applied in practical, everyday situations?

7. Consider the notion of the old self being "crucified" in baptism (Romans 6:1–6). What does this signify about the depth of transformation expected in a believer's life?

8. How does the continuous renewal of our minds (Ephesians 4:23) play a crucial role in living out our Christian faith?

9. In the contrast between the Gentile's futility of thinking and the believer's renewal in the spirit of their mind, what does this tell us about the power of our thought patterns on our spiritual health?

10. Discuss the importance of living out the values of God's kingdom, such as love, forgiveness, and hope, together with others. How does spiritual adoption influence our relationships and interactions with fellow believers and the broader world?

Lesson 3

Spiritual Family

Loyalty to Christ, Each Other,
and the Local Church's Mission

Before You Begin

Read Ephesians 2:12–19; 4:1–6.

Pray for those in your local congregation, including the elders and other spiritual leaders. Pick out a few members who may be hurting, struggling spiritually, or needing to become more connected to the local body and pray for them.

Introduction

When a child is adopted into a new family, they often go from tragic circumstances and family dysfunction into a new situation of stability. In their old situation, they may have been orphaned, neglected, or abused. They often find stability, peace, and love in their new home. Their parents have committed to caring for, protecting, and nurturing that child as it grows into adulthood. On top of that, that child gets *a family*. Maybe it's brothers, sisters, aunts, uncles, grandparents, and friends. It's a beautiful thing.

Spiritually, when God adopts us, we go from total separation (foreigners and strangers) to the household of God. I love the imagery in Ephesians 2 where Paul says the Gentiles weren't just invited to God's house; they got a seat at God's table (2:12–19). Through the work of Christ, God is bringing people together from every tribe, every nation, every language, and every culture and making them one. Paul likens this to a building being put together and growing *into a holy temple in the Lord. In him, you are also being built together for God's dwelling in the Spirit* (2:21–22). Your coming into the body of Christ is not just about you—it is Christ and the new family of fellow believers you receive.

Today, our world often emphasizes individual spirituality and the pursuit of personal faith. Because of this, the essential nature of the local church within the Christian life cannot be overstated. The New Testament presents a clear picture: when a person comes to Christ, he or she receives a new spiritual family: the church. The notion of experiencing salvation outside the context of a local church community is entirely foreign to the New Testament. Our Lord Jesus Christ, throughout His teachings and through the establishment of His church, assumed that believers would not live their faith in isolation but within a family of like precious faith.

Paul's letters to the early churches emphasize this concept. In his greetings to the Corinthians, (1 Corinthians 1:1–2), Paul addresses individuals *and* a collective body of believers, sanctified in Christ Jesus and called to be saints together. Similar greetings can be found in his letters to other churches, such as those in Galatia and Corinth again (Galatians 1:2; 2 Corinthians 1:1). These passages highlight the early church's nature as a local body of worshiping saints, highlighting the Lord's design for His followers to belong to individual congregations.

Ephesians 1:22–23 and Ephesians 5 reveal Christ's relationship with the church. He is its head, and it is His bride, the object of His supreme love and affection. Paul writes:

> Husbands, love your wives, just as Christ loved the church and gave himself for her to make her holy, cleansing her with the washing of water by the word (Ephesians 5:25–26).

Acts 20:28 reminds us of the immense value Jesus places on the church, having shed His blood for it. Our Lord's deep love and commitment should inspire us to value and commit to our local congregation profoundly and personally.

Why Being a Part of a Spiritual Family Is So Important?

A Matter of Obedience

First and foremost, it comes down to obedience: The New Testament indicates that believers were baptized and gathered into local churches, often with their names recorded. In 1 Peter 5:1–2, local church members are identified as the flock. The shepherds of each church knew who each member was. This was not a casual affiliation but a committed identification with a local church body. History tells us when they moved from one place to another, and a letter often accompanied them so that a transfer might happen to another local assembly. Examples of this practice include Apollos in Acts 18:27 and Phoebe in Romans 16:1–2, demonstrating the early church's orderly and committed nature (see the example of Mark in Colossians 4:10). There was never an assumption that a Christian would be floating around alone. The Biblical pattern points to a fundamental unity of saved souls.

A Matter of Fellowship

The New Testament's emphasis on fellowship shows believers shared spiritual life and common faith:

> God is faithful; you were called by him into fellowship with his Son, Jesus Christ our Lord (1 Corinthians 1:9).

> What we have seen and heard we also declare to you, so that you may also have fellowship with us; and indeed our fellowship is with the Father and with his Son, Jesus Christ (1 John 1:3).

This fellowship was not superficial. Instead, it was a deep, participatory sharing in the life and mission of the church. Mutual care, worship, and encouragement, as detailed in Hebrews 10:22–25, exemplify the vital role of collective gatherings in nurturing the Christian's faith and love.

> Let us draw near with a true heart in full assurance of faith, with our hearts sprinkled clean from an evil conscience and our bodies washed in pure water. Let us hold on to the confession of our hope without wavering since he who promised is faithful. And let us consider one another in order to provoke love and good works, not neglecting to gather together, as some are in the habit of doing, but encouraging each other, and all the more as you see the day approaching.

A Matter of Identity

Each church member is united with Christ (Galatians 2:20) and thereby with each other in an incredible spiritual family. In this, we see a collective belonging to the body of Christ, of which we are all integral parts (Ephesians 4:1–6). Our shared identity in Christ forms the foundation of our unity and mutual commitment.

In the opening verses of Ephesians 4, Paul shows us what this looks like in the life of the local congregation:

- 4:1—Every member is dedicated to being who they've been called to be in Christ. This is what it means to walk worthy.
- 4:2—Every member adopts the attitudes of *humility, gentleness, patience, and bearing with one another in love.* These attitudes are like the glue that holds us all together.
- 4:3—Every member makes it the highest priority to maintain the unity the Spirit provides by striving for peace. It is no longer about our self-interests but what is good for the body.
- 4:4–6—These are the things upon which all Christians are to agree. They serve as things we rally behind as Christians as they make up the core of Christian doctrine.

As a Matter of Loyalty

The church is depicted as a family, a community where loyalty and mutual support are paramount (Ephesians 2:19). In a world where individual interests often prevail, the New Testament calls us to a loyalty that prioritizes the well-being of our spiritual brothers and sisters and the collective mission of the local church.

What's In This for Us?

Commit to a Local Church. We need to see the importance of being part of a local church. We're not talking about casual affiliation but a committed identification with a loving group of people where you can be nurtured, grow, and also contribute to the growth of others. Just as a child adopted into a new family finds stability and love, being part of a church family provides spiritual stability, love, and a sense of belonging. It's a place to exercise obedience and fellowship, find identity, and express loyalty within the body of Christ.

Engage in Deep, Meaningful Fellowship. The New Testament highlights the depth of fellowship within the church—a sharing of life and mission. This involves more than just attending services; it's about engaging in mutual care, encouragement, and worship. It's participating in a shared spiritual life, provoking one another to love and good works, and supporting each other's faith and mutual growth, especially as we anticipate Christ's return.

Embrace Your Identity in Christ. Recognize that your adoption into God's family redefines your identity. You're called to live this out in unity and peace with fellow Christians, contributing to the church's mission. This involves adopting attitudes of humility, gentleness, patience, and love, strengthening the bonds within the local church.

Prioritize Unity and Peace. Paul urges every church member to prioritize maintaining unity and peace. This unity is not based on our efforts but on the Spirit's work within us. It requires setting aside personal interests for the greater good. As part of a local congregation, your loyalty is to Christ, each other, and the local church's mission. This is how we reflect Christ's love and commitment to the world.

Conclusion

The local church is where obedience, fellowship, identity, and loyalty converge, creating a dynamic environment for spiritual growth. By recognizing the value of our spiritual family, we embrace the fullness of the Christian life, grounded in God's love and purpose as revealed in His Word.

For Reflection

1. How does the practice of adoption into a new family help us understand our relationship with God and the church?

2. How does being part of a local church challenge the modern emphasis on individual spirituality?

3. Discuss the importance of fellowship in the church. How does it go beyond being in the same space to sharing each other's lives and missions?

4. What role does obedience play in our participation in the local church, and why is it considered a matter of obedience to be part of a church community?

5. How does the New Testament's depiction of the church as a body of believers challenge our contemporary understanding of church membership and attendance?

6. In what practical ways can church members build the attitudes of humility, gentleness, patience, and love that Paul describes in Ephesians 4?

7. How does our identity in Christ influence our interactions and unity within the local church?

8. Discuss the concept of loyalty within the church. How does prioritizing the well-being of our spiritual brothers and sisters and the church's mission reflect the teachings of the New Testament?

9. Reflect on the statement, "The church is not an optional add-on to our life but is the very context in which our faith is lived out, nurtured, and brought to fulfillment." How does this perspective challenge or affirm your current involvement and commitment to your local church?

Lesson 4

Gifted, Godly Leaders

Empowering the Local Church:
Unveiling the Role of Spiritual Leaders

Before You Begin

Read Ephesians 4:7–13.

Pray for an open mind and heart to receive the Word with humility and receptiveness. Pray a prayer of thankfulness for the spiritual leaders God has put in your life, for greater appreciation of their role, and for their desire to support and encourage you in your spiritual life.

Introduction

> And he himself gave some to be apostles, some prophets, some evangelists, some pastors, and teachers, to equip the saints for the work of ministry, to build up the body of Christ (Ephesians 4:11–12).

Previously, we have explored what happens in our spiritual adoption—how we have been transferred from spiritual isolation to belonging to God's family (Colossians 1:12–14), marked by a new identity and a set of values rooted in love and unity. Now, we will learn about another remarkable characteristic of our adoption: the invaluable presence of godly, gifted leaders in the local church.

In Ephesians 4:11–12, the apostle Paul unveils a divine design for the spiritual edification of our spiritual family. He reveals that Christ Himself has bestowed upon His church a group of leaders—each endowed with unique gifts and roles—who are instrumental in equipping and empowering the body of Christ for the work of service, leading to its growth and maturity.

In this lesson, we will discover the significance of spiritual leadership in the church's life and its profound impact on our individual and collective spiritual growth. We will explore the roles these leaders fulfill, the power of their ministry, and the principles of servant leadership they exemplify. I hope our hearts are stirred with gratitude for the leaders God has graciously placed in our midst and that we are inspired to actively participate in building up the local church we are part of.

Why God Has Given Us Leaders

In Ephesians 4, Paul presents a call to action for the Christian—"walk worthily." This command forms the basis for Christian living, urging us to conduct our lives in a manner that aligns with our newfound identity in Christ. This is not a passive acceptance of salvation but an intentional pursuit of righteousness and holiness.

In verses 2 and 3, Paul elaborates on what this worthy walk entails, outlining key attributes such as humility, gentleness, patience, forbearing love, and unity. These virtues are essential marks of the Christian life, shaping our interactions and reflecting Christ's character to the world. Furthermore, Paul identifies the foundational principles of this worthy walk in verses 4 to 6. He speaks of the "seven ones"—unity in the Spirit, the Son, and the Father –the bedrock of our faith and practice. In essence, our walk in unity with God and fellow believers is inseparable from our identity as children of God.

Next, to empower the Christian to walk worthily, Paul highlights the abundant resources available to us in verses 7–11. First, he reminds us of the personal gift received from Christ upon salvation, abundantly providing us with the necessary grace and spiritual enablement to live victoriously. Additionally, Paul emphasizes the role of leaders within the church—who serve as conduits of God's grace and wisdom. We need to see and appreciate them for what they are: divine gifts bestowed upon the church by Christ Himself.

In understanding their significance, it's crucial to recognize their purpose and mission. They have been called to work diligently for the spiritual growth and maturity of those under their charge. Evangelists and shepherds, in particular, are entrusted with nurturing believers toward full maturity in Christ, guiding them in becoming more like their Savior.

We Could Summarize Ephesians 4:1–11 in This Way

- 4:1—Live the life.
- 4:2–3—How to live the life.
- 4:4–6—The foundation of the life.
- 4:7–11—The resources for living the life.

Our Leaders Equip Us

> to equip the saints for the work of ministry, to build up the body of Christ (Ephesians 4:12).

The God-given task of evangelists, teachers, and pastors is to promote our spiritual growth and maturity in Christ and His Word. Their role extends beyond filling up church buildings or providing programs and entertainment. Instead, their primary focus is guiding individuals toward spiritual stability and maturity in their faith. This purpose aligns with Paul's exhortation to the Corinthians as expressed in 2 Corinthians 13:11.

> Become mature, be encouraged, be of the same mind, be at peace, and the God of love and peace will be with you.

The mission of those who serve us is centered on building growth, stability, enthusiasm, unity, and peace within the local church.

Moreover, true spiritual leaders approach their ministry with passion. For them, it is not just a profession. They understand how they have been called to dedicate themselves fully to their work, wholeheartedly expending their energy and efforts. As highlighted in Colossians 1:28, their proclamation of Christ is accompanied by warnings and teachings, delivered with wisdom acquired through deep thought, study, prayer, and discernment.

> We proclaim him, warning and teaching everyone with all wisdom, so that we may present everyone mature in Christ.

Their teaching isn't reactionary; it is strategically designed to fulfill God's purposes, which requires time and discipline. Our leaders have no off-hours; their commitment extends to wrestling in prayer, as seen in the example of Epaphras in Colossians 4:12, who tirelessly interceded for believers' spiritual maturity and assurance. Thus, their dedication and passion are indispensable in guiding us toward maturity in Christ and fulfilling God's will.

How Leaders Equip the Church

The Continual Teaching of Sound Doctrine

This is emphasized throughout scripture as essential for our spiritual growth and edification. In 2 Timothy 4:2, Paul instructs Timothy to preach the Word faithfully, regardless of circumstances, and to correct, rebuke, and encourage with great patience and teaching. Similarly, in 1 Timothy 4:6, Paul emphasizes the importance of pointing out the truths of the faith, nourishing those in the church with sound teaching. The point is to continually instruct, bring forward, and lay the truths of scripture before the church with gentle, humble persuasion, ensuring that our leaders think biblically and apply biblical principles in their teaching.

Constant Reproduction of Mature Believers

Paul's exhortation to Timothy in 2 Timothy 2:2 emphasizes the importance of passing on sound teaching to faithful individuals who will, in turn, teach others. Likewise, in 2 Timothy 2:15, Timothy is urged to diligently present himself as one approved by correctly teaching the word of truth. This commitment to training rightly and adequately reflects the dedication of elders, ministers, and teachers to nurturing spiritual growth and maturity in the church.

Set an Example

Shepherds, ministers, and teachers are called to set an example for believers. In 1 Timothy 4:11, Timothy is commanded to teach and command with authority. The effectiveness of this instruction lies in the consistency between the leaders' lives and the message they preach. They diligently read, explain, and apply scripture, ensuring that their lives align with the truths they proclaim.

Teach the Whole Plan of God

This is another vital aspect of biblical leadership. As seen in Acts 20:27, leaders do not hold back from declaring the entirety of God's truth, even when specific topics may be sensitive or controversial. This commitment to faithfully proclaiming God's Word is essential because, as Acts 20:28

illustrates, elders are appointed by the Holy Spirit to shepherd and care for the church purchased with Christ's blood.

Equipping Brings Unity

Equipping the local church for ministry is central to the role of our leaders, as stated in Ephesians 4:12. The word "equip" implies completing or perfecting the saints, building unity, understanding, and conviction among them. This equipping work aims to unite us in fellowship, ministry, admonishment, confession, and forgiveness, thereby maintaining unity within the local congregation. Ultimately, our leaders work tirelessly to create an atmosphere conducive to spiritual growth and unity, ensuring the ongoing health and vitality of the local church.

What's In This for Us Today?

1. Teaching sound doctrine is essential for spiritual growth and edification (2 Timothy 4:2, 1 Timothy 4:6).
2. The role of leaders is to continually instruct, persuade, and apply biblical principles in teaching (Ephesians 4:11–12).
3. Leaders are tasked with constantly reproducing mature believers (2 Timothy 2:2, 2 Timothy 2:15).
4. Setting an example is crucial for leaders, ensuring consistency between their lives and the message they preach (1 Timothy 4:11).
5. Teaching the whole plan of God, even sensitive or controversial topics, is essential. (Acts 20:27–28).
6. Equipping the local church brings unity, understanding, and conviction among church members (Ephesians 4:12, 1 Corinthians 1:10).
7. The goal is to build spiritual growth, maturity, and unity within the local church.

Conclusion

This lesson has been designed to help you see the significance of godly, gifted leaders in the local church and their indispensable role in facilitating spiritual growth, maturity, and unity. Through the continual teaching of sound doctrine, reproduction of mature believers, setting of examples, and faithful proclamation of the whole plan of God, our leaders *equip the saints for the work of ministry, building up the body of Christ*. As we reflect, may we appreciate the invaluable presence of our ministers, elders, and teachers and actively participate in the collective work of building up the local church. Let us continue to support, honor, and pray for our leaders as they diligently serve God and His people, striving toward the unity, growth, and maturity of the body of Christ.

For Reflection

1. How does understanding the role of spiritual leaders in the church impact your personal growth and spiritual life?

2. Reflect on when a leader's teaching or example significantly influenced your faith. What lessons did you learn from that experience?

3. How can you support and encourage your local congregation's ministers, elders, and teachers?

4. Consider the qualities outlined in Ephesians 4:2–3 (humility, gentleness, patience, forbearing love, and unity). How can you embody these attributes in your interactions with others within the local church?

5. What steps can you take to grow your understanding of sound doctrine and biblical principles?

6. How can you actively participate in the elders' mission of bringing you to maturity in Christ?

7. Reflect on the example-setting aspect of spiritual leadership mentioned in 1 Timothy 4:11. How can you strive to set a positive example for others in your walk of faith?

8. Think about instances where you've experienced unity and understanding within the local church. What factors contributed to these positive experiences, and how can you cultivate them?

9. How can you contribute to the ongoing work of equipping the saints for ministry and building up the body of Christ within your local church context?

Lesson 5

Freedom from Sin

Set Free from Satan's Bondage, Living for a Glorious Future

Read Colossians 2:11–14; Romans 6:1–12.

Pray for God's help in embracing your freedom in Christ and for more strength in living out your calling in daily life.

Introduction

I love Paul's writing in Colossians 2:11–14:

> You were also circumcised in him with a circumcision not done with hands, by putting off the body of flesh, in the circumcision of Christ, when you were buried with him in baptism, in which you were also raised with him through faith in the working of God, who raised him from the dead. And when you were dead in trespasses and in the uncircumcision of your flesh, he made you alive with him and forgave us all our trespasses. He erased the certificate of debt, with its obligations, that was against us and opposed to us, and has taken it away by nailing it to the cross.

Before God adopted you, you were dead in your sins and trespasses and separated from Him. Your sins had piled up before Him, and there was no way you could repay the debt you owed—except by eternal death. When you chose to call upon His name by responding to the gospel invitation, God *made you alive with him and forgave (you) all (your) trespasses.* At the moment of your baptism, the debt you owed was canceled. You are no longer obligated to pay it—because Jesus took your debt of sin away, nailing it to the cross. Oh, how precious is our adoption! Without Him, we would be hopelessly lost, under sin, and eternally doomed.

Satan's primary objective is to lie. He is the father of lies (John 8:44). Every day, through every means possible, he works to convince us that sin is not serious. He tells us it has no consequences and won't hurt anyone; no one else will ever find out. *You deserve it. It's OK to do it just once and then never again. You only live once. You need to have fun and not be so dull.* On and on his lies go.

Yet, the Bible warns that sin is a direct offense against God's holiness and righteousness, and it carries devastating consequences. Its catastrophic impact affects our present existence and eternal destiny. Sin creates an impassable divide between us and God, hindering our relationship with Him. It brings brokenness, pain, and suffering into our lives and those around us.

When we consider the weight of sin and the consequences of eternal separation, our greatest need is redemption. The Bible makes it clear that the soul that sins will die (Ezekiel 18:20) and that sin is of the devil (1 John 3:8). Our redemption requires divine intervention and the destruction of the works of the devil, which Jesus accomplished through His death (Colossians 2:13–15).

The redemption of a person's soul results from God's unparalleled wisdom, immeasurable love, and unrivaled power. There is no more remarkable example of love, mercy, or knowledge than what was demonstrated in the sacrifice made to bring salvation to humanity. Likewise, there is no more fantastic display of power than what the Holy Spirit accomplishes in resurrecting a dead soul to life. Through the power of the Holy Spirit, individuals who were once spiritually dead experience new life and transformation. We can only find proper redemption and restoration through God's wisdom, love, and power. The fact that our rescue required the supreme effort of divinity is indisputable evidence of our utmost need for salvation.

The whole purpose of Christianity is our redemption. Therefore, its mission is ultimately optimistic. *For God did not send his Son into the world to condemn the world, but to save the world through him* (John 3:17). Isaiah 35 says:

> The wilderness and the dry land will be glad; the desert will rejoice and blossom like a wildflower. It will blossom abundantly and will also rejoice with joy and singing. The glory of Lebanon will be given to it, the splendor of Carmel and Sharon. They will see the glory of the Lord, the splendor of our God. Strengthen the weak hands, steady the shaking knees! Say to the cowardly: "Be strong; do not fear! Here is your God; vengeance is coming. God's

retribution is coming; he will save you." Then the eyes of the blind will be opened, and the ears of the deaf unstopped. Then the lame will leap like a deer, and the tongue of the mute will sing for joy, for water will gush in the wilderness, and streams in the desert; the parched ground will become a pool, and the thirsty land, springs. In the haunt of jackals, in their lairs, there will be grass, reeds, and papyrus. A road will be there and a way; it will be called the Holy Way. The unclean will not travel on it, but it will be for the one who walks the path. Fools will not wander on it. There will be no lion there, and no vicious beast will go up on it; they will not be found there. But the redeemed will walk on it, and the ransomed of the Lord will return and come to Zion with singing, crowned with unending joy. Joy and gladness will overtake them, and sorrow and sighing will flee.

Christianity is centered on the good news of salvation and offers hope and deliverance from the bondage of sin. In carrying out the mission, God calls upon us to trumpet the greatest blessing, freedom from sin's enslavement, leading to unadulterated joy. This lesson will explore the freedom from sin that your spiritual adoption provides. This is one of the most critical lessons in this book.

Your Past: Enslaved to Sin

Perhaps the best passage that explains our former condition and compares it with our new status in Christ is Romans 7:11:

> For sin, seizing an opportunity through the commandment, deceived me, and through it killed me.

Notice how Paul personifies sin as a powerful enemy that attacks and kills us. Satan uses God's law as his tool of deceit. He lies to us, saying that God's law is a restraint to what we deserve and hides its life-giving purposes from us. He stirs resentment toward God, making us question His motives for prohibiting certain things as we seek self-fulfillment.

Another good passage to consider is found in Paul's writing in the previous chapter:

> For we know that our old self was crucified with him so that the body ruled by sin might be rendered powerless so that we may no longer be enslaved to sin (Romans 6:6).

When controlled by sin's potent grip, our flesh is known as the "body ruled by sin." This term signifies a body overwhelmed and maneuvered by sin, serving as a launching pad for various temptations and unbridled desires. Under such influence, individuals find themselves steered by carnality, allowing these base instincts to override moral discernment and to be pursued without restraint. Paul calls it "the body of death" in Romans 7.24 to refer to the physical body not merely in terms of mortal death but as an entity trapped in spiritual demise. How he describes it in Ephesians 2:1–3 also sheds light on our former condition:

> And you were dead in your trespasses and sins in which you previously walked according to the ways of this world, according to the ruler of the power of the air, the spirit now working in the disobedient. We too all previously lived among them in our fleshly desires, carrying out the inclinations of our flesh and thoughts, and we were by nature children under wrath as the others were also.

Your Present: Free From Sin

Before you were saved, you were subject to the *law of sin and death*. Sin was the dominant power over your life, and death was its outcome. Wherever sin rules, death always comes (Romans 6:23). The two are inseparable and inescapable by human power. But now, because of your adoption in Christ, you have been set free! Paul says it so well in Romans 8:1–4:

> Therefore, there is now no condemnation for those in Christ Jesus because the law of the Spirit of life in Christ Jesus has set you free from the law of sin and death. For what the law could not do since it was weakened by the flesh, God did. He condemned sin in the flesh by sending his own Son in the likeness of sinful flesh as a sin offering, in order that the law's requirement would be fulfilled in us who do not walk according to the flesh but according to the Spirit.

Despite the presence of sin in our lives leading us to commit actions we regret, we have the assurance that these sins won't lead to condemnation because of Christ's sacrifice. We are justified through Christ's death, freeing us from any punishment. Life's hardships are not divine penalties, and we face no eternal damnation post-death, with the promise of resurrection mitigating the fear of death itself. Through Jesus Christ, the influence of the Spirit of life has replaced the dominance of sin and death over our lives. The key message in this context is that Christ's atoning sacrifice has broken the rule that sin leads to death, justifying those who have fallen short.

As we contend with sin's relentless challenges, it's crucial to remember that Christ has severed the link between sin and death, liberating us from condemnation. In our pursuit of sanctification, we should maintain focus and be supported by doubts concerning our initial salvation.

Now, Free From Anxiety and Confusion: You Live for Christ

Since we are sons and daughters, we must always pay attention to the responsibility that comes with our new status. God has recreated you *to be holy and blameless in love before him* (1:4). *This is our daily pursuit for the rest of our lives* here on earth.

Let's look at 2 Corinthians 7:1. First, Paul says we have been given promises. Go back to 6:16.

> And what agreement does the temple of God have with idols? For we are the temple of the living God, as God said: I will dwell and walk among them, and I will be their God, and they will be my people.

Here, we have the promise of a close and meaningful relationship with God and status. The Christian belongs to God. We are His *people*. This is an act of grace. In response, we are called to *come out from among them and be separate* (6:17). Our work (obedient response) should always be seen in response to what has or continues to do for us by grace. Since we belong to Him, we must draw a line with the world and no longer participate in its deeds.

Then Paul repeats the pattern. Verse 18: I will be a father to you, and you will be sons and daughters to me. God did this for you. You did not save yourself. Since you are saved, you cleanse yourself from every impurity of the flesh and spirit, bringing holiness to completion in the fear of God (7:1b).

Fear here means reverence and respect. You don't cower in fear because your status (adopted, forgiven, and holy) is uncertain or tenuous; you demonstrate tremendous respect (and love) for God by living inside the new responsibilities you've been given. Remember, you work from salvation — not for it.

You are His workmanship (Ephesians 2:10). You are His *masterpiece.* God wants to be glorified through you. He is glorified when we live for Him. As you walk with Him daily, the spirit bears with your spirit that you are a child of God. We should all be humbled by what God has done. Because of His work, let us lift Jesus every day in every way we can. God is incredible and amazing. Praise Him for His marvelous grace!

What's in This for Us?

Embrace Your New Identity in Christ: Recognize and live out the truth that, through faith and baptism, you have been given a new identity. This means leaving behind the past dominated by sin and embracing the freedom Christ's sacrifice offers. Just as Paul highlights in Colossians 2:11–14, your old self, enslaved to sin, has been replaced with a new self, alive in Christ and freed from sin's penalty. This calls for a daily commitment to reject sin's lies and embrace the holiness and righteousness you are named as a child of God.

Understand the Process of Sanctification: The lesson from Colossians and the subsequent teachings make clear that salvation is both an event and a process—justification being the event and sanctification the ongoing process. Sanctification requires diligent effort, cooperating with the Holy Spirit's work within you to grow in holiness and resist sin's temptations. This journey of sanctification is lifelong, requiring patience, perseverance, and continual reliance on God's grace. Engage actively in practices that build spiritual growth, such as prayer, studying scripture, and participating in the life of your local congregation, recognizing that freedom from sin's power is progressively realized as you walk in obedience to God.

Proclaim the Message of Redemption and Hope: The ultimate purpose of Christianity, as the lesson illustrates, is redemption and the restoration of all creation. This hopeful message is not just for personal comfort but is to be shared with the world. You are called to share this good news with others because you have been freed from sin's enslavement and granted eternal life through Christ. This involves verbal proclamation and living out the gospel daily, demonstrating the power of Christ's love through your actions, relationships, and service to others. Doing so, you participate in God's redemptive mission, bringing hope and light to those still walking in darkness.

Conclusion

In conclusion, Paul's Colossian writings are a powerful reminder of our transformation from sin to salvation through Christ. As sons and daughters of God, we are called to embrace our new identity, deeply rooted in the freedom Christ secured for us on the cross. This involves recognizing our liberation from sin's penalty and actively engaging in the process of sanctification—whereby we grow in holiness and resist the deceptive allure of sin under the guidance of the Holy Spirit.

Moreover, our redemption compels us to be ambassadors of hope, sharing God's love and the promise of eternal life with a world in desperate need of salvation. Living out our faith authentically and proclaiming the gospel through our words and deeds brings glory to God.

We have been called to live lives marked by grace, transformation, and a steadfast commitment to the gospel. Freedom in Christ is not an end but a means through which we are empowered to serve, love, and lead others to the same hope we have found.

For Reflection

1. How does understanding the distinction between justification, sanctification, and glorification change one's view of one's spiritual life?

2. In what ways have you experienced the reality of being freed from the penalty of sin through Christ's sacrifice?

3. How can sanctification be seen in your daily life, and what practices help you grow in holiness?

4. Reflect on when you felt the power of sin weakened in your life. What role did faith and the Holy Spirit play in that transformation?

5. What does living out your new identity in Christ mean to you personally in a world that often contradicts Christian values?

6. How can the hope of glorification and eternal life with God motivate you to persevere through trials and temptations?

7. How can you more effectively share the message of redemption and hope with those around you?

8. Consider the impact of viewing Christianity as a set of beliefs and a mission of redemption. How does this perspective influence your purpose and daily actions?

9. Reflect on the statement, "We work from salvation, not for it." How does this truth affect your understanding of grace and efforts to live a holy life?

10. How does the promise of no condemnation for those in Christ Jesus provide comfort and confidence in your spiritual walk, especially during times of struggle or doubt?

Lesson 6

A Peace Not Like the World

Navigating with Faith and Contentment

Read: Philippians 4:1–13; John 14:27.

Pray for God's help in developing a deeper understanding of how the peace of God works in your life.

Introduction

In his book *Confessions,* Augustine prayed: *You made us for yourself, and our hearts find no peace until they rest in you.* Perhaps it was Paul Augustine had in mind when he penned those words, for it was Paul who lived this out in an authentic way:

> And the peace of God, which surpasses all understanding, will guard your hearts and minds in Christ Jesus. Finally brothers and sisters, whatever is true, whatever is honorable, whatever is just, whatever is pure, whatever is lovely, whatever is commendable— if there is any moral excellence and if there is anything praiseworthy— dwell on these things. Do what you have learned and received and heard from me, and seen in me, and the God of peace will be with you. I rejoiced in the Lord greatly because once again you renewed your care for me. You were, in fact, concerned about me but lacked the opportunity to show it. I don't say this out of need, for I have learned to be content in whatever circumstances I find myself. I know how to make do with little, and I know how to make do with a lot. In any and all circumstances I have learned the secret of being content—whether well fed or hungry, whether in abundance or in need. I am able to do all things through him who strengthens me (Philippians 4:7–13).

This may be one of Paul's most significant works. He captures the heart of spiritual focus, contentment, and peace, all built on the foundation of Jesus Christ.

As you reread this text, note first how peace is a guard that protects our hearts and minds. It works most effectively as we dwell on true, honorable, just, pure, lovely, and commendable things. God works to provide us with peace. We cooperate and submit to His will. This is how God is the God of peace.

Paul knew from personal experience that God is the *God of peace.* Every need he had was met every time—whether in circumstances of need or abundance. Paul possessed the ultimate confidence that God was with him. In verse 12, he says he has learned the secret of being content and found true peace. True peace comes when we do not allow our circumstances to impede our influence and activity in the kingdom. In other words, it comes when we entirely devote ourselves to God and ultimately depend on His resources. This is why Paul could write down the words that so many of us have memorized: *I am able to do all things through Him who strengthens me.* Paul understood that no matter what came upon him, good or bad, persecution or abundant blessing, he would be given the strength to fulfill God's purposes.

I believe what we have in Philippians 4:7–13 describes his literal experience with true peace — a peace that comes to us from outside this world — the peace that will calm troubled hearts.

Where did Paul get this peace?

Paul felt, I believe, the fulfillment or actualization of what Jesus spoke of in John 14:27:

> Peace I leave with you. My peace I give to you. I do not give to you as the world gives. Don't let your heart be troubled or fearful.

The peace that Jesus leaves is what enabled Paul *and every Christian:*

- To fight back fear.
- To rejoice amid trial.
- To sing while suffering.
- To stand with the most tremendous confidence in the face of death.

The peace that Jesus provides is the gift of an attitude that impacts every part of life. It is so much more than the absence of trouble. Which, by the way, is a fabrication. In this life, there are hardly any moments where we do not have some problem. *There is always something.* Paul's secret in Philippians 4:12 comes from a higher source — one outside this world. What Jesus brings to us is never impacted by circumstances. It is, however, a peace that can and will affect our circumstances and bring glory to Christ.

John 14:27a—Defining True Peace

In scripture, two types of peace are defined: objective and subjective. The first may be described as a state of peace, while the other is the experience of peace. Both come from a supernatural source. We will only discover the *experience* of peace once we are first brought into a *state* of peace.

Romans 5:1–11—A State of Peace

Paul writes:

> Therefore, since we have been justified by faith, we have peace with God through our Lord Jesus Christ (Romans 5:1).

"Peace," as found here, is the removal of hostility between God and us. The Christian is no longer at war with God. Our rebellion ceased at the cross. Our sins have been forgiven. Now, we move from the perspective of hope and assurance, 5:4–5. Think of it. We have gone from enmity and war against God to now having God dwell in us. *If anyone loves me, he will keep my word. My Father will love him, and we will come to him and make our home with him,* John 14:23. Perhaps Paul summarized it best at the end of the first section of Romans 5. In verses 10–11, he says that we have received *reconciliation.* The Christian lives in a state of peace with God.

Colossians 1:20–29—What Brought About Our Peace?

Notice Colossians 1:20. The present state of peace we enjoy was made *through His blood, shed on the cross.* And now, look at 1:22. Because of this reconciliation, Jesus presents you to His Father as *holy, faultless, and blameless.* These are qualities you presently possess as a Christian. You have, are, and will stand justified in the sight of God. You have been set free from condemnation, Romans 8:1. You have been, *and will be,* delivered from the wrath to come, 1 Thessalonians 1:10.

Indeed, we must remember that the work of Jesus entails an inherent responsibility. In Colossians 1:23, Paul speaks of the need for our continuous cooperation with God, whereby we allow Him to ground us and make us steadfast so that we will not be shifted away from the hope of the gospel. We must be committed to spiritual maturity (1:28). As we grow, we work by the strength Christ gives us (1:29).

We need to understand better how the strength of Christ is powerfully at work in us and that the state of peace we enjoy is not precarious. It is not unstable. Because of the righteousness Jesus has brought us and given us through His death and our acceptance of it through faith, we have peace with God.

John 14:27—The Experience of Peace

The peace Jesus brings is positive. It is so optimistic that it literally can impact the circumstances in which we live. It goes on offense to keep our hearts from swaying throughout life. This is the peace Paul was speaking of in Philippians 4:7:

> And the peace of God, which surpasses all understanding, will guard your hearts and minds in Christ Jesus.

Here, it is the *peace of God,* not peace with God. And again, see how it is aggressive in that it attacks whatever situation we're in, finding joy through Christ. You can see it in the preceding verses in Philippians 4:

- It fueled the joy Paul expressed in 4:4.
- It was the source of his graciousness in 4:5.
- It was behind the active prayer life referenced in 4:6.
- It is the following through in total confidence in 4:19.

Again, see how Paul's peace does not come from his circumstances—it existed over them, helping Paul to frame his experiences from a spiritual perspective.

Philippians 4:7—Peace Serves as a Guard

"Guard" in this verse comes from a military word that means to stand at a post and guard or protect against enemy aggression. Peace stands guard at the door of your heart against the corrosive acid of worry. It stands over our minds, fighting against unworthy and inaccurate thoughts that wreak havoc on them.

What kind of self-talk do you engage in? For many, the ongoing narrative they have with themselves is a collection of lies. "I'll never be good enough."

"I always fail." "I just wasn't meant to succeed." "No one cares about me." "I'm alone." "No one cares about me or my problems." These thoughts can go on with reckless abandon. And we must take these thoughts captive to the obedience of Christ, 1 Corinthians 10:4–5. Until we do, we will never have peace. This may be one of the avenues where Satan is most effective against us. While he has all sorts of options to attack us from the outside, he renders most of us inactive before we get out the door every morning by all the lies he says through our negative self-talk.

If you want this peace, you must first make peace with God. Once you have that, you experience peace based on faith.

- In your past. You're not guilty — and stand forgiven, Romans 5:1.
- In your present. You *stand by grace,* Romans 5:2.
- In your future, you are no longer dominated by fear—your eternal destination has been determined, and your status as a son or daughter of God is never precarious (Romans 5:5).

John 14:27b–The Source of Peace

Jesus says *my peace I give to you.* There is no other source of true peace. No earthly source of peace ever lasts. There is always something over the horizon. But the peace that the Bible speaks of is from God.

- Philippians 4:9—God is the God of peace.
- Hebrews 7:2—Jesus is the King of peace.
- Galatians 5:22—by His fruit, the Spirit produces peace.

True peace comes from God—those without God will not find peace without Him. Look again at John 14:27. Jesus gives us peace. How? By the work of the Spirit, 14:23, 27. In John 16:14, the Spirit takes the things of Christ and gives them to us. He brings life, instruction, and peace.

Whose Peace Does Christ Bring?

Jesus says He brings *my peace.* The same peace that filled Him as He was mocked, tortured, and killed is given to us. It works. He used it in the greatest battle in the hours leading up to and on the cross. He promises that when He leaves, He will give the Christian this peace. Think of how this peace has helped you:

- Find peace in times of danger.

- Experience calm in trouble.
- Gain freedom from anxiety.

In this way, the peace He brings is aggressive in that it helps us tackle our troubles or challenges. When dealing with the most significant problems, we are well rooted, have a strong foundation, and are like a rock — because we stand on the rock. The peace Jesus possessed was undistracted fearlessness. It was total trust. It was dependence on God. Read John 19 and see how Pilate stood in amazement at Jesus' disposition during the most extreme circumstances. This is the kind of peace that He supplies you with.

This Is Not the Peace the World Gives

The world does not have peace. It prays for peace … but searches for it in all the wrong places. The only peace the world offers is an escape from reality. Some try to find it in all the wrong places and wind up wrecking their lives because it never satisfies them. All the trouble comes back — with even more trouble piled up on top— after one is forced to come back to reality the morning after, coming down from the high or having to pay the bill.

The world can't find peace because it does not know God. It's not circumstances, family history, or past mistreatment. If a person lacks peace, they have either a troubled or no relationship with God. *There is no peace for the wicked, says the Lord* (Isaiah 48:22). The only way to make peace is to make peace with God.

John 14:27c—The Impact of Peace

Don't let your heart be troubled or fearful. Peace has been given to you, but you must receive it and apply it to your life. How much do you believe in God? How much will you trust Him? Especially as you think about your future—because this is usually what generates most of your anxiety. Some people struggle with their past, but the future often concerns them the most. So, will we choose to remember that everything is under the care of our God?

This is how peace is to impact our life. We constantly remember:

- He has forgiven our past.
- He is with us in the present.
- He has secured our future.

So, as Jesus says, don't let your heart be troubled or fearful.

What's in This for Us?

Cultivate a Spiritual Perspective: How concentrated is your focus on things that are true, honorable, just, pure, lovely, and commendable? Are you consciously directing your thoughts and actions towards these virtues? This involves recognizing what aligns with these qualities and actively incorporating them into your daily life. When you do this, you guard your heart and mind, allowing God's peace to thrive within you.

Learn Contentment in Every Situation: Paul's example teaches the secret of being content in any circumstance, relying on Christ's strength. Practically, this means shifting your source of satisfaction from external conditions to your relationship with Christ. Whether you face abundance or need, you can experience peace by trusting in God's provision and timing, recognizing that your ultimate fulfillment comes from Him.

Embrace Peace as a Way of Life: Jesus's peace differs from the world's temporary solutions. It requires us to make peace with God through faith, acknowledging the reconciliation made possible by Jesus's sacrifice. In daily life, this peace involves rejecting fear and anxiety, especially about the future, and trusting in God's care. This mindset transforms how you face life's challenges, enabling you to experience true peace that influences your circumstances rather than being overshadowed by them.

Pursue a Relationship with God as the Foundation of Peace: The ultimate source of peace is a relationship with God, facilitated by Jesus Christ and empowered by the Holy Spirit. To apply this, prioritize your spiritual health through prayer, reading Scripture, and fellowship in the local church. This deepens your understanding of God's character and promises, helping you be anchored in peace regardless of life's storms. By maintaining a close relationship with God, you ensure that your peace is not just a fleeting emotion but a lasting state of being that reflects your trust in Him.

Conclusion

The same man who wrote *I can do all things through Him who strengthens me*, also wrote:

> We are afflicted in every way but not crushed; we are perplexed but not in despair; we are persecuted but not abandoned; we are

struck down but not destroyed, for we who live are always being given over to death for Jesus' sake, so that Jesus' life may also be displayed in our mortal flesh (2 Corinthians 4:8–9, 11).

How did he do it? How did he win? *How can we win?*

Paul elevated his focus:

> For our momentary light affliction is producing for us an absolutely incomparable eternal weight of glory. So we do not focus on what is seen, but on what is unseen. For what is seen is temporary, but what is unseen is eternal (2 Corinthians 4:17–18).

We must learn to turn our attention away from the problem and look to the eternal. We must turn the focus off ourselves and focus on Jesus. The strength is not in you but in Christ Jesus, who lives in you. I can do all things through Him who strengthens me. This is the peace Jesus left for Paul. It's the peace Jesus left for you.

For Reflection

1. How does Augustine's statement that "our hearts find no peace until they rest in you" resonate with your experiences of seeking fulfillment and peace in life?

2. In what ways does the peace of God act as a guard over your heart and mind, as described in Philippians 4:7? Can you share a personal example?

3. Reflecting on Paul's words in Philippians 4:8, how can you focus on true, honorable, just, pure, lovely, and commendable things that impact your daily life and thought processes?

4. Paul speaks about learning to be content in all circumstances. What practical steps can you take to cultivate contentment, especially in difficult times?

5. Discuss the difference between the peace of the world and the peace that Jesus offers, as mentioned in John 14:27. How have you experienced this difference in your own life?

6. Paul's ability to be content and at peace regardless of his circumstances is central to his message in Philippians 4:7–13. What role does faith play in achieving such peace and contentment?

7. Making peace with God is the foundation for experiencing true peace. How do you understand this process, and what has been your journey toward making peace with God?

8. Considering the aggressive nature of the peace of God described in Philippians 4:7, how can we actively engage this peace in our struggles with fear, anxiety, and uncertainty?

9. How can we practically "guard" our hearts and minds to maintain peace in a world full of chaos and trouble?

10. Paul's strength and peace came from his focus on the eternal rather than the temporary. How can we shift our focus from our immediate circumstances to God's eternal promises in our daily lives?

Lesson 7

A Different Outlook on Life

Life from an Eternal Perspective

Before You Begin

Read: Ephesians 2:11–22; 2 Corinthians 5:11–17.

Pray for better understanding and a more significant commitment to leading life from a spiritual perspective. Express your thankfulness to God for the new life He has given you through Christ, and ask Him for help in your spiritual growth and progress to greater maturity.

Introduction

The power of Jesus is seen in Ephesians 2:11–22, which reveals the essence of our spiritual renewal. Before coming to Christ, we were in a state of spiritual deadness, alienated from the citizenship in His kingdom, devoid of hope, and absent from God. This bleak existence demonstrates our desperate need for salvation.

Thankfully, Christ intervened, and His sacrifice allowed us to be near Him. After our spiritual adoption, His proximity is not only about being closer physically or emotionally; it involves a fundamental change in our spiritual status. We have become fellow citizens with the saints and gain access to the Father, which elevates us from our previously hopeless state to one of dignity and promise.

This access brings us deeper communion, where we become part of God's household, sharing fellowship with Him. The magnitude of this transformation is striking—once outsiders, we are now embraced as God's children. This new identity is a testament to the impact of divine grace, reminding us of our origins and the grace that defines our new identity.

Understanding the depth of our former alienation—with its sheer hopelessness and the destructive nature of sin—highlights the severity of our past and the necessity of redemption. Sin, with its soul-corroding power, traps us in a cycle of despair, emphasizing our incapacity to save ourselves and pointing to our need for a greater force to rescue us from our self-inflicted predicaments.

Realizing our dire need for God is crucial to the transformation process. Encountering Him allows us to see life from a new perspective. As discussed thus far in this study, our adoption redefines our priorities, and our lives become centered around Jesus. We experience transformation through Christ's power, where old ways dissipate and new life begins.

In this lesson, we will explore how our relationship with Jesus redefines who we are and how we live, offering us a new perspective and an invigorated sense of purpose. The goal is to understand further the life-changing power of our faith and the continual renewal it brings.

What Motivated Paul in His Mission

2 Corinthians is Paul's defense of his integrity, written in response to the challenges he faced from dishonest false teachers who sought to discredit him. These adversaries were vigorous in their efforts, pushing him into a delicate situation where he felt compelled to defend himself to preserve the effectiveness of his ministry. However, he knew the danger of appearing self-serving, arrogant, or prideful.

In navigating these challenges, Paul transparently revealed his motives for ministry throughout 2 Corinthians. A prime example of this approach is in 2 Corinthians 6:11, where he states, "We have spoken openly to you, Corinthians; our heart has been opened wide." Paul wanted the Corinthians to examine his heart, recognize his integrity, and acknowledge the purity of his motives.

Leading up to this, Paul outlined several motives that drove his work. These are seen in detail in 2 Corinthians 5:11–17.

- In 5:11, he emphasizes his reverence for the Lord, which was the foundation of his devotion and faithful service.
- In 5:12, he expresses a constant concern for the unity and witness of the church, highlighting the power of genuine and sincere hearts in testifying to the lost.
- In 5:13, his devotion to truth is evident—even to the point where his fervent passion led some to claim he was insane. His passionate

preaching, driven by his convictions and divine inspiration, underscores his commitment to God and his followers.

Now, we will go further into Paul's writings, specifically looking at 2 Corinthians 5:14–15 and 5:17, exploring how the sacrifice of Jesus impacted Paul and, by extension, affects us. These passages illuminate how God rejuvenates and transforms lives through the power of Jesus' sacrifice, offering a new perspective from which to live. This transformation is central to understanding the depth of change that the gospel brings into the lives of believers, continually renewing them in the image of Christ.

The Love of Christ Propels Us

> For the love of Christ compels us, since we have reached this conclusion, that one died for all, and therefore all died. And he died for all so that those who live should no longer live for themselves, but for the one who died for them and was raised (2 Corinthians 5:14–15).

Paul's encounter with Christ's overwhelming love is the cornerstone of his theological reflection and ministerial motivation. His love was not just a theological abstract but a reality; Jesus died for him while he was still entrenched in sin, specifically for Saul of Tarsus, the notorious persecutor of Christians. Jesus' sacrificial death was not just a general act of redemption but *a personal exchange*—His life for Saul's. This act was not due to Saul's merits but was a manifestation of Jesus' magnanimous, unmerited love. This love compelled and drove Paul to dedicate his life to serving others.

This overwhelming love should not be exclusive to Paul; it extends to all of us. The same love that transformed Saul into Paul should also move us deeply, compelling us to reflect on our past and recognize the complete contrast to where we stand now in Christ. *For the love of Christ compels us*, this love should govern our actions and decisions, exerting a pressure that results in measurable Christian action.

We must fully surrender to Jesus, allowing His love to control every facet of our lives. This idea is further seen in 2 Corinthians 5:14b, which reminds us that *one died for all, and therefore all died*. This shows us how our lives are no longer centered around our desires but are instead focused on Christ and His will. Our gratitude for His sacrifice should be evident in our dedication to living for Him, as Paul emphasizes by the continuation of his thoughts in 2 Corinthians 5:15:

> And he died for all so that those who live should no longer live for themselves, but for the one who died for them and was raised.

Our old selves have died, and now we live for Christ.

This is seen in other New Testament writings.

- Galatians 2:20 elaborates on this new existence: "I have been crucified with Christ and I no longer live, but Christ lives in me. The life I now live in the body, I live by faith in the Son of God, who loved me and gave himself for me."
- This idea of substitution and transformation is also reflected in 1 Peter 2:24, emphasizing that Christ's death enables us to die to sin and live to righteousness. We are a new creation, in-dwelled and empowered by the Spirit.

This goes far beyond initial salvation from eternal damnation; it is a complete overhaul of our nature and purposes, as described in Titus 2:13–14:

> While we wait for the blessed hope, the appearing of the glory of our great God and Savior, Jesus Christ. He gave himself for us to redeem us from all lawlessness and to cleanse for himself a people for his own possession, eager to do good works.

Jesus' sacrifice aims not just to save us from hell but to purify us, making us righteous people who actively live out His will and purposes. Thus, the Christian life is about embodying the love of Christ, living a life hidden with Christ in God, as stated in Colossians 3:3, and moving forward in faith and righteousness, empowered by the Holy Spirit.

The Old Has Passed Away

> From now on, then, we do not know anyone from a worldly perspective. Even if we have known Christ from a worldly perspective, we no longer know him this way. Therefore, if anyone is in Christ, he is a new creation; the old has passed away, and see, the new has come! (2 Corinthians 5:16–17)

From the moment we believe, we are called to walk in the newness of life. This fundamental change is particularly evident in how Paul shifted his view of others. Previously, he might have assessed people based on worldly standards like physical appearance, superficial behavior, or personality traits. However, following his conversion, Paul ceased recognizing people "according to the flesh," as noted in 2 Corinthians 5:16a. External judgments no longer clouded his interactions; instead, he viewed life through a lens enriched with spiritual insight and divine wisdom.

This viewpoint is behind what it means to become a "new creation." The impact of Jesus' death and resurrection promises that anyone, regardless of past transgressions or status—from the most notorious sinners to societal outcasts—can be remade. This offers new knowledge, wisdom, and a shift in priorities from the temporary to the eternal, changing how individuals see themselves and others. It cultivates a vision that sees beyond earthly attributes to each person's more profound spiritual connections with God.

I think Paul further elaborates on this idea by emphasizing our security in Christ, suggesting that being "in Christ" provides a reformation of identity and an assurance of our future with Him. Jesus guarantees our eternal inheritance, accessible exclusively to those who find their identity in Him.

The term "new creation" carries significant weight in Paul's epistles, as he uses it in various contexts to describe the radical change brought about by Christ's salvation. For example, in Galatians 6:15 and Ephesians 4:24, Paul speaks of God's desire to recreate us in Christ and the call to put on the new self, respectively.

> For both circumcision and uncircumcision mean nothing; what matters instead is a new creation (Galatians 6:15).
>
> And to put on the new self, the one created according to God's likeness in righteousness and purity of the truth (Ephesians 4:24).

This concept was not unfamiliar to Paul's audience; in the Old Testament, Jews used the term to describe someone whose sins were forgiven. Paul adapts this term to describe Jesus's comprehensive work in our salvation.

Ultimately, being a new creation in Christ is not only about personal renewal; it's about living in a way that reflects our deepened relationship with God. As we die to our old selves and live through Christ, we are not only transformed individually but are also given the power to view and interact with the world around us from this refreshed sanctified perspective. This shift affects every aspect of our lives and guides us to live according to our new, divine nature.

A Reality in Process

God is actively involved in our salvation, personally investing His effort and energy into transforming our lives. As He works within us, our old ideas, plans, values, loves, passions, principles, and beliefs are profoundly changing. It's important to note that this transformation does not imply we become sinless; instead, God instills new desires, inclinations, appetites, truths, and values aligned with His will.

As we nurture and develop these new traits, they begin to overpower our old, fleshly tendencies, and we gradually transform into the image of Jesus. However, this process requires our full cooperation and surrender. We must not resist or hold back the changes God wants to make in us; He can only work to the extent we allow Him. A vital aspect of this involves shifting our view of Christianity—from focusing on what we must give up to embracing what we gain in Christ.

Upon coming to Christ, we begin to reevaluate everything. As we do, our perception of what is essential should change. Suppose we find ourselves clinging to old ideas, values, or passions. In that case, it indicates a lack of complete surrender to God. 2 Corinthians 5:17c emphasizes that "the new has come," using a verb tense that implies a continuing state of fact, indicating that our growth is ongoing and enduring.

Our new state brings about a new perspective on time and eternity. As adopted sons or daughters of God, we no longer live for the temporal but for the eternal. Now, we see reality more clearly. Despite living in the world, we live from a new viewpoint, rejecting worldly standards, motives, judgments, and values.

> So if you have been raised with Christ, seek the things above, where Christ is, seated at the right hand of God. Set your minds on things above, not on earthly things (Colossians 3:1–2).

The old ways are gone, and we are called to focus on God's perfect standard of holiness. While we may only partially meet this standard, it is our goal and guide. Pursuing holiness reshapes our lives, prompting us to live according to God's divine standards rather than the world's.

What's In This for Us?

Embrace total transformation: Your spiritual renewal goes far beyond external changes. It involves actively nurturing new desires and inclinations that align with God's will. This involves a profound internal shift that allows us to transform into Jesus's image gradually. Each day, choose to build these godly traits over your old habits and fleshly desires, recognizing that this is ongoing and requires continuous dedication.

Prioritize eternal perspectives over temporary views: As we realize the importance of living for eternity rather than just for the present, we must adjust our priorities and values accordingly. This shift in focus helps us evaluate life's situations, opportunities, and challenges from a spiritual perspective, ensuring that our actions and decisions are anchored in eternal truths, not just immediate gratifications or pressures.

Live for Christ in everyday interactions: Deciding to no longer live for ourselves, we live for Christ who died for us, calls for a daily commitment to reflecting Christ's love and grace in our interactions. Whether at work, at home, or in the local community, our lives should be testimonials of the power of Christ's love, seeking to serve others and promote unity and righteousness as Paul did.

Continuously evaluate and surrender: Regular self-assessment of our spiritual life is vital to ensure we are not clinging to old patterns or resisting the Spirit's work. Surrendering to His work involves letting go of previous identities, values, and priorities that conflict with our new identity in Christ. This might mean reevaluating relationships, career choices, or personal goals to ensure they align with our Christian faith and values.

Conclusion

What have we learned here?

When we fully embrace Christ's life, we will experience a new existence where our old selves are replaced by new creations defined by godliness, purpose, and an eternal perspective. Our daily lives should be a living testament to the grace and renewal found in Christ. By committing to a life that continuously seeks God's standards over worldly ones, nurturing new spiritual inclinations, and prioritizing eternal values, we draw closer to God and become living illustrations of His power in a world that desperately needs hope. How strong is your commitment to live fully for Him? Are you embracing every opportunity to demonstrate His love and truth in all you do?

For Reflection

1. How does understanding our previous state of spiritual deadness enhance our appreciation of Christ's sacrifice?

2. In what ways have you personally experienced transformation since accepting Christ into your life? Share specific changes in values or perspectives.

3. Paul talks about not evaluating others "according to the flesh." How can we apply this principle in our daily interactions with people?

4. Discuss how being a "new creation" impacts our identity and actions. Can you think of a moment when this became particularly clear to you?

5. How does the idea that "the love of Christ compels us" influence our motivation for service and ministry? Share an example where this love guided your decisions or actions.

6. What old desires or passions have you had to surrender to embrace the new life Christ offers fully? How did you go about making these changes?

7. How can we practically "set our minds on things above" daily? Discuss strategies that have worked for you, or that could work.

8. What does living "not for ourselves but for Him who died for us" mean? How does this perspective change our roles in our families, workplaces, and communities?

9. Discuss the importance of continuous spiritual evaluation. What practices help you stay aligned with God's will and be aware of any areas needing surrender?

10. How can the local church support its members in transforming and living out their new identity in Christ? What roles do accountability and fellowship play in this process?

Lesson 8

A Different Outlook on Death

*Living with Purpose:
Embracing Each Day as a Gift from God*

Before You Begin

Read: Psalm 90:12; Hebrews 9:27; Philippians 1:20–23; 2 Timothy 4:6–8.

Pray more thankfulness for the precious gift of each day that God grants. Pray for help in restoring strained relationships or unresolved conflicts in your life. Ask God to heal your damaged relationships and give you the strength to seek reconciliation. Ask God for guidance on living out your purpose—using your talents and resources for His glory.

Introduction

Teach us to number our days carefully so that we may develop wisdom in our hearts (Psalm 90:12).

One day, you will die. It's a cold reality, but it's the truth. We don't like to think about this. It is easy to see how everyone else is headed that way, but it is hard to envision the reality for ourselves. Have you ever returned to your high school class reunion, looked around the room, and stared? *Who are all these old people?* They're doing the same thing and thinking the same thing about you. It has been said there are three stages to life: youth, middle age, and finally, "My, you're looking great today." All of us are somewhere along that continuum.

As you read Psalm 90:12, the writer stresses that we do not count the days … but make the days count. What is called for is for us to lead a life of significance—living outside of ourselves. This is what it means to *live like you are dying*. How would it change your life today if you received word that tomorrow, next month, or next year would begin without you? Would it change your priorities?

Would you be thinking more about your relationship with God? *Are you ready to meet Him face to face?* This is life's priority. In the end, nothing matters but this. Hebrews 9:27 says you will die, judgment will come, and your eternal destiny will be realized.

Would you be thinking more about your relationships with those you love? Are there any situations you need to repair? Who would you need to thank, apologize to, extend forgiveness, or remind that you love them? Before you go, you want to clear up those things as much as possible.

Would you embrace excellence by rejecting mediocrity and complacency? Would you be true to yourself, embracing the talents you have? Would you bloom where you're planted and do what you could for others in the place you are? Would you concentrate on what you have, not what you don't, and use all you have to serve others? Would you do it with urgency, knowing that every day, every hour, is precious?

Would you work to approach death positively? No one wants to head into death with regret. I believe everyone wants to head into eternity without regret, saying *I lived my life well.* We all want to be like Paul, who got to the end and said:

> There is reserved for me the crown of righteousness, which the Lord, the righteous Judge, will give me on that day, and not only to me, but to all those who have loved his appearing (2 Timothy 4:8).

Paul approached his death with confidence, assurance, and hope. He demonstrated a spirit of positivity and optimism. So, *how do we get there?*

In this lesson, we'll learn how.

Your Life Belongs to God

> The life of every living thing is in his hand, as well as the breath of all humanity (Job 12:10).

God made you. You belong to Him by His creation. Your life is not your own. *In him we live and move and have our being* (Acts 17:28). Your breath is in the hand of God (Daniel 5:23). The sooner we can figure this one fact out in life, the better our life will be. Your life is not your own; *it belongs to God.*

Since this is true, we must not waste our lives. At best, it is uncertain and fragile. It may end at any moment—whether we are young or old. It is very possible to waste a life. Jesus said that one's life does not consist of *the abundance of his possessions* (Luke 12:15). The person who lives like he is dying understands this. Accumulating things is not what this life is for. No sane person on his deathbed ever found comfort in his possessions. It is scary to think that we could take the one-time gift of life and squander it. But it happens. All around, we see people who gave in to addiction and destroyed their lives through drugs and alcohol. Countless people die in the commission of a crime. A life can end in seconds.

But it's not just about life ending in tragedy. Americans have a mindset of preserving comfort, safety, security, and ease … at all costs. There is no better illustration than how culture shapes our view of retirement. The cultural view is that people should have 20–30 years of leisure and pleasure. The image is of healthy older people living in Florida or Arizona who are busy living in an RV, fishing, cruising, golfing, playing bingo or shuffleboard, and living with no thought whatsoever about the reality of waking up on the other side face to face with Jesus and his nail-scarred hands. When they retire, some people retire from everything, including the Lord. That is retirement *wasted*.

Instead, may we all make the radical decision to walk another way so that when we advance to an older age, with fire in our bones, we say, "I am, with my remaining energy, going to pour out my life for God and His kingdom." The last thing a person would want to hear is, "You fool, how did all that pointless play bring glory to my name?"

Life is a Gift to Display the Image of Christ

This should be the goal of every person's life: to display Christ's infinite value for the world. Your possessions have been given to you so that you can demonstrate that Jesus is your pleasure—not your things. Money, things, and treasure have been given to you so that they may be used in service of the kingdom. Your passion—in everything—is to magnify Christ.

What was Paul's passion?

> My eager expectation and hope is that I will not be ashamed about anything, but that now as always, with all courage, Christ will be highly honored in my body, whether by life or by death (Philippians 1:20).

For Paul, nothing else mattered but that Jesus be honored, i.e., that He be made to look like the treasure He is. That's why you have life—to bring glory to God. This is to be the driving force behind every decision.

Whether by Life

Do we count *everything as a loss* for the *surpassing worth of knowing Christ* (Philippians 3:7–8)? Money, houses, land, cars, computers—everything we have needs to be used to show Jesus as more valuable than things. Family, friends, and even your life should be used for His glory. *How do we do that?* By treasuring Christ above all. We must make the life choices that demonstrate this fact.

Whether by Death

Paul said, in Philippians 1:21, that *death is gain.* How? It is far better to *depart and be with Christ,* 1:23. When Jesus is more satisfying to you than all life can give, being with Him at death will be gain. Death will be gain to us when:

- Our life is lived to display the supreme value of Christ.
- We treasure Jesus above all earthly things and persons.
- We are willing to take risks and sacrifice to enjoy Him more.

This is what Paul could say:

> I take pleasure in weaknesses, insults, hardships, persecutions, and in difficulties, for the sake of Christ. For when I am weak, then I am strong (2 Corinthians 12:10).

Paul would do whatever it took to magnify Jesus—including personal pain and sacrifice.

How You Can Approach Death Positively

> For I am already being poured out as a drink offering, and the time for my departure is close. I have fought the good fight, I have finished the race, I have kept the faith. There is reserved for me the crown of righteousness, which the Lord, the righteous Judge, will give me on that day, and not only to me, but to all those who have loved his appearing (2 Timothy 4:6–8).

If you were reading verse 7 out of Young's Literal Translation, it would say:

The good fight I have fought.

The course I have finished.

The faith I have kept.

The Fight

If we were to transliterate Paul's fighting the good fight, he would say, "I have agonized the agony." In other words, he sustained maximum effort in his struggle for victory. He struggled mightily with his flesh and all its problems of lust, laziness, and misplaced priorities. He engaged in daily combat with Satan. In Colossians 1:29, he said he had "labored unto weariness."

Notice also how he calls it the "good" fight. What he engaged in was a noble calling. The calling we have received from God is noble and high. You have been chosen for the task of working to spread the message of reconciliation. You are an ambassador of Christ (2 Corinthians 5:19–20). Your spiritual work is the best thing you can do in life.

The Course

Paul had the discipline to stay on track. The time you stay off the course is time lost. What are some things that can knock you off course? There are many, but let's focus on two for a moment:

- The unnecessary baggage you choose to carry throughout life. This could be harboring resentment, holding on to hurt, picking up worldly habits, or *anything* that distracts you from the mission of loving God and others.
- Sin.

Since these things are true:

> Therefore, since we also have such a large cloud of witnesses surrounding us, let us lay aside every hindrance and the sin that so easily ensnares us. Let us run with endurance the race that lies before us, keeping our eyes on Jesus, the pioneer and perfecter of our faith. For the joy that lay before him, he endured the cross, despising the shame, and sat down at the right hand of the throne of God (Hebrews 12:1–2).

The Faith

Paul lived under the authority of the Word. He finished his responsibilities toward God. He says *he kept* the faith. This was written in present-perfect tense, demonstrating a past action with continuing results. He is saying that, throughout his life, he had done these things until they had been finished.

What Can We Learn From This?

Here is Paul at the end of his life, with no regrets. There is no sadness, remorse, or sense of un-fulfillment. There is no sense of being incomplete. The closest I've ever experienced something like this is with my dad. My dad died on the Friday before Christmas in 2013. Earlier that week, on Monday, we had our last private conversation. He talked about his life, and I remember him saying he was ready to go. He had done all he could do. He knew where he was going. He had no regrets. When you get to this moment, you only have *trust and hope*. What I remember most as we talked was his absence of worry and no regret. There was just simple trusting, abiding faith.

This was despite the fact he had yet to be perfect. My dad would be the first to speak of his many failures—but in the end, he was still committed—he was still fighting—and *he was as strong as he had ever been spiritually*—even though his body was the weakest it had ever been. For Dad, he died without even a hint of the most minor thing being undone.

Indeed, this was the way it was with Paul:

- What God called him to do—he did.
- What God equipped him to do—he did.
- What God allowed him to do—he did.

And by this, he faced death with genuine satisfaction. He died triumphantly—a life's work completed.

This should be our goal. It's what we've been called to do. It's the way God is preparing you to leave this world. Are you committed to:

- Doing what God calls you to do?
- Trusting in God's equipping you as you serve?
- Going where God presents you with the opportunity to go?

What's In This for Us?

Live intentionally for eternal values: Understanding the fleeting nature of life as highlighted by Psalm 90:12, strive to live a life that reflects significance and purpose beyond earthly achievements. This includes building relationships, serving others, and engaging in activities that align with eternal values rather than accumulating material possessions.

Prioritize relationships and reconciliation: As you contemplate your mortality, it's crucial to prioritize relationships, make amends where necessary, express gratitude, and offer forgiveness. This ensures you leave no regrets or unresolved issues, building peace and love with family and friends.

Embrace excellence in all endeavors: Reject mediocrity by fully utilizing the talents and opportunities God has given you. Strive to excel in your personal and professional life, not for personal glory but to honor God through your work and interactions, showcasing the power of living a Christ-centered life.

Prepare positively for the end: Inspired by Paul's example in 2 Timothy 4:6–8, approach the end of life with confidence and hope. Engage in spiritual disciplines that strengthen your faith and character, ensuring that you can face death without regret, having lived a life that glorifies Christ in all aspects.

Conclusion

Will you focus your life on the temporary, such as accumulating material wealth or building bigger barns, or will your primary endeavor be to lay up treasures in heaven? Will you seek the fleeting approval and praise of men? Or will you choose a path that leads to enduring fulfillment by making Jesus the all-satisfying treasure of your life?

For Reflection

1. What does it mean to "number our days" according to Psalm 90:12, and how can this perspective change your daily priorities?

2. As you reflect on the idea that "one day you will die," how does this reality influence your decisions and interactions with others?

3. How can you shift your focus from accumulating possessions to building lasting relationships and spiritual wealth?

4. Discuss how living like you are dying can lead to a life of greater purpose and significance. What changes might you need to make to live this way?

5. How can we ensure our relationships with loved ones are in good standing without waiting for the urgency of life's final moments?

6. What does embracing excellence look like in your day-to-day life? How can you reject mediocrity and complacency in a practical sense?

7. Paul talks about being poured out as a drink offering at the end of his life (2 Timothy 4:6–8). How can you apply this metaphor to your spiritual life?

8. How can you demonstrate that Jesus is more valuable than your possessions or achievements?

9. How can the fear of death or the end of life be transformed into a positive force in your Christian walk?

10. Discuss practical steps to prepare spiritually for your eventual meeting with God. What does this preparation look like in everyday life?

Lesson 9

Spiritual Confidence

Unshakable Faith in God's Eternal Promises

Before You Begin

Read: Revelation 2:9–11; Romans 7:14–19, 25—8:2; 8:38–39.

Pray for help to broaden your understanding and assurance of God's promises in His word and help you live more confidently in His truth. Ask for help softening doubts so you can face life's challenges with a steadfast belief in God's walking alongside you.

Introduction

Be faithful to the point of death, and I will give you the crown of life (Revelation 2:10).

What an incredible verse! Do we understand what it means? Let's look at another passage from Revelation:

Then I heard a loud voice in heaven say, The salvation and the power and the kingdom of our God and the authority of his Christ have now come, because the accuser of our brothers and sisters, who accuses them before our God day and night, has been thrown down. They conquered him by the blood of the Lamb and by the word of their testimony; for they did not love their lives to the point of death (Revelation 12:10–11).

In verse 11, the word *conquered* stands out. Victory was theirs *by the blood of the lamb* and their steadfastness, perseverance, and faithfulness. They were confident that everything God promised would be true *for them*. This made them commit to God personally and meaningfully, trusting He was connected to them.

Now, let's go back to Revelation 2:9–11 and note Jesus' very personal connection to the church in Smyrna:

> I know your affliction and poverty, but you are rich. I know the slander of those who say they are Jews and are not, but are a synagogue of Satan (Revelation 2:9).

See how Jesus *knew their physical circumstances.* He knew about their suffering. He is not aloof, distant, or uncaring. It is as if He is right there with them, suffering alongside them. He reminds them that they *are rich.* These are tender words of encouragement to enrich, strengthen, and bolster their faith. Spiritually, Jesus says they were in abundance. They had every resource they needed. For the church at Smyrna, believing God and taking Him at His word, pushing through and holding out, demonstrated the quality of their faith.

> Don't be afraid of what you are about to suffer. Look, the devil is about to throw some of you into prison to test you, and you will experience affliction for ten days. Be faithful to the point of death, and I will give you the crown of life (Revelation 2:10).

Here, Jesus says, *don't be afraid of what you're about to suffer.* He then says *you will experience affliction.* Now that's sobering. What if Jesus came to you and told you that? Would you be ready? Are you sufficiently rooted to withstand that kind of storm? The truth is that Christ and His apostles have already come to us through the word and warned us about suffering and affliction. It's all a test from Satan. We must remember that all the trials Satan puts before us are temporary and will come to an end. But while we're in the middle of it, we must remember we are never alone, have access to the strength or power God provides as He walks with us, and find solace in the victory to come.

> "Let anyone who has ears to hear listen to what the Spirit says to the churches. The one who conquers will never be harmed by the second death (Revelation 2:11).

The one who conquers will live eternally. This is the life that matters and the one you must not miss.

The point of this lesson is to live in a way that frames everything in this life for the next. Achieving this perspective requires a profound level of cooperation and surrender to God. As we commit to this process, allowing God to guide our steps, our trust and confidence in Him naturally grow. This deepening faith challenges us to consider whether we are truly rooted in our spiritual lives.

Are we embodying the traits of a strong Christian? If we were to observe a strong Christian, we would likely see robust habits—devotion to God and fellow saints, consistent prayer, diligent study of scripture, and active engagement in positively impacting others. As suggested in Philippians 4:8, their thoughts dwell on whatever is true, noble, proper, pure, lovely, and admirable.

For the next few moments, I want you to know that we will focus specifically on confidence, an essential attribute of strong Christians. We will discuss the importance of trust, where to place it, and how to cultivate it. More importantly, we will explore how this confidence supports us throughout life, offering resilience and stability no matter our challenges. This is about acknowledging the necessity of confidence and understanding how it can be actively developed and maintained in our daily walk with Christ.

The Vital Importance of Being Confident in Our Faith

First, it must be understood that we are not talking about arrogance … but confidence in God, His word, and His promises. Note what Paul said:

> Therefore, my dear brothers and sisters, be steadfast, immovable, always excelling in the Lord's work, because you know that your labor in the Lord is not in vain (1 Corinthians 15:58).

It should be our goal to be steadfast. Immovable. To excel as a Christian. Again, this is not arrogance but a quiet confidence or trust in God that propels us into daily action in executing Christian duty. Here's another passage to consider from Ephesians:

> Then we will no longer be little children, tossed by the waves and blown around by every wind of teaching, by human cunning with cleverness in the techniques of deceit (Ephesians 4:14).

We're not to be like "little children." Instead, we are to know what God wants us to do. Spiritual knowledge comes from the *maturity* of the previous verse. Is it possible to be sure of what God wants? It certainly is. This is particularly comforting as we live in a time where we receive so many conflicting messages that the enemy designs to raise questions and doubts. Satan has made it popular to believe that the only sure thing is *that you can't be sure*. Can we know everything in the Bible is correct? The answer is yes! How? *By faith.*

Are you willing to stake your soul's survival on it?

Paul did. He knew what he was doing and how he was living was correct. He says:

> And that is why I suffer these things. But I am not ashamed, because I know whom I have believed and am persuaded that he is able to guard what has been entrusted to me until that day (2 Timothy 1:12).

If you aren't confident, you aren't strong.

Confidence is a cornerstone of spiritual strength and being deeply rooted in faith. We need confidence to grapple with doubt and insecurity about fundamental aspects of our faith, such as our forgiveness and eternal destiny. It's not uncommon to encounter Christians wrestling with these doubts. Many find themselves fluctuating in and out of faith, struggling with habitual sins, and feeling disconnected from their local church family—infrequently attending services or spending time with their brothers and sisters. These struggles are not just about lacking faith but also about lacking the confidence that strengthens and sustains it.

Take, for example, Peter's early experiences. There were moments in his life, like during the storm on the sea in Matthew 14 and the night before Christ's death, where his confidence faltered significantly. His fear, anxiety, and doubt led to actions driven by self-preservation, focusing solely on the immediate threats rather than the bigger picture.

What happened to Peter demonstrates why confidence is vital, especially as we live the Christian life in a world that often contradicts godly values. As Christians, we are, metaphorically, going upstream in a downstream world. We face the challenge of acting modestly in an immodest world and striving for a life of purity amidst pervasive sinfulness. Jesus said:

> The light has come into the world, and people loved darkness rather than the light because their deeds were evil (John 3:19).

This environment means we will inevitably face scrutiny, questioning, and often unpleasant interactions. We must be reminded of our calling in such a world.

- Philippians 2:15 encourages us to be "blameless and pure, children of God who are faultless in a crooked and perverted generation, among whom you shine like stars in the world."
- 1 Peter 4:14 reassures us, "If you are ridiculed for the name of Christ, you are blessed, because the Spirit of glory and of God rests on you."

These passages highlight the stark contrast between Christian living and worldly values and the inevitability of not "fitting in" with the world.

So, confidence is not just a personal trait but a spiritual necessity. It equips us to handle the difficulties and opposition we encounter as we live out our faith. Building and maintaining this confidence is essential for navigating the challenges of a life committed to Christ, ensuring we can stand firm no matter what we face.

How Can We Gain Confidence?

Trust the Word

Trusting the Word of God is the foundation for building strong faith and conviction, which builds courage and confidence. More study and profound understanding lead to greater conviction, propelling us to act because we know what is right. Often, people question how one can preach with such confidence and live with certainty about their salvation, wondering if it borders on arrogance. Yet, studying God's Word solidifies our trust, as it continually presents promises of assurance.

In the Word are Continual Promises of Assurance

The assurances found in scripture affirm that what God promises is indeed true. He has established a covenant with us, urging us to trust in His saving grace, love, and mercy, even though we are often weak and sinful. For example, the Apostle Paul openly discusses his struggles in Romans 7, acknowledging human nature and the internal conflict it creates. Despite his best intentions, he often found himself doing the things he hated, a struggle many of us can relate to. Yet, Paul never grew comfortable with sin; instead, he despised it and strove to overcome it.

> For we know that the law is spiritual, but I am of the flesh, sold as a slave under sin. For I do not understand what I am doing, because

> I do not practice what I want to do, but I do what I hate. Now if I do what I do not want to do, I agree with the law that it is good. So now I am no longer the one doing it, but it is sin living in me. For I know that nothing good lives in me, that is, in my flesh. For the desire to do what is good is with me, but there is no ability to do it. For I do not do the good that I want to do, but I practice the evil that I do not want to do (Romans 7:14–19).

This ongoing battle with sin highlights the importance of not becoming content with our sinful tendencies. We have made a covenant with God to resist the flesh and persevere in our faith. While perfection is unattainable as long as we are in the flesh, it is not our perfection but our heart's posture toward God that matters most. Living under constant guilt about our performance can erode our confidence and lead to discouragement and defeat. It's crucial to recognize that while we strive to avoid sin, as Paul did, we are covered by grace when we fail.

You Have Been Set Free

Thankfully, we have been set free from the law of sin and death through Christ Jesus.

> Thanks be to God through Jesus Christ our Lord! So then, with my mind I myself am serving the law of God, but with my flesh, the law of sin. Therefore, there is now no condemnation for those in Christ Jesus, because the law of the Spirit of life in Christ Jesus has set you free from the law of sin and death (Romans 7:25—8:2).

Your freedom allows you to approach God's throne boldly, knowing that you have an advocate in Jesus Christ who intercedes for you when you sin (1 John 2:1–3). This is a fantastic source of comfort and confidence, as emphasized in Hebrews 4, where we are encouraged to come boldly before the throne of grace to receive mercy and find help in our time of need.

> Therefore, let us approach the throne of grace with boldness, so that we may receive mercy and find grace to help us in time of need (Hebrews 4:16).

Trust the Father

In Romans 8, Paul poses several rhetorical questions that underscore our security in Christ's love, which nothing can sever. He asks:

- If God is for us, who is against us? (v. 31)
- How will He not also with Him grant us everything? (v. 32)
- Who can bring an accusation against God's elect? (v. 33)
- Who is the one who condemns? (v. 34)
- Who can separate us from the love of Christ? (v. 35)

What God has promised is true:

> For I am persuaded that neither death nor life, nor angels nor rulers, nor things present nor things to come, nor powers, nor height nor depth, nor any other created thing will be able to separate us from the love of God that is in Christ Jesus our Lord (Romans 8:38–39).

Nothing in all creation can separate us from God's love in Christ Jesus our Lord. This promise assures us of God's unfailing love and the surety of our salvation.

Trust the Spirit

By trusting in the Spirit, as outlined in Romans 8:14, 16, we are reminded that we are God's children and that the Spirit Himself affirms this truth.

> For all those led by God's Spirit are God's sons.

> The Spirit himself testifies together with our spirit that we are God's children,

The Spirit also aids us in our weaknesses and intercedes when we are unsure what to pray for.

> In the same way the Spirit also helps us in our weakness, because we do not know what to pray for as we should, but the Spirit himself intercedes for us with inexpressible groanings (Romans 8:26).

This continual divine support strengthens and comforts us, ensuring that our confidence does not rest on our imperfect selves but is rooted in Christ and God's assurance through His Spirit.

Confidence Helps You Through Life

It helps you:

As you walk

If we walk in the light as he himself is in the light, we have fellowship with one another, and the blood of Jesus his Son cleanses us from all sin (1 John 1:7).

In What You Say

but in your hearts regard Christ the Lord as holy, ready at any time to give a defense to anyone who asks you for a reason for the hope that is in you (1 Peter 3:15).

In Your Prayers

This is the confidence we have before him: If we ask anything according to his will, he hears us (1 John 5:14).

In the Future

because I know this will lead to my salvation through your prayers and help from the Spirit of Jesus Christ. My eager expectation and hope is that I will not be ashamed about anything, but that now as always, with all courage, Christ will be highly honored in my body, whether by life or by death (Philippians 1:19–20).

We live in an uncertain world. As we face the prospect of living in a nation in decline, extreme moral decay, world war, and economic destruction, *we will have help from the spirit of Jesus Christ.* No matter what happens, we know God will be with us.

What's in This for Us?

Embrace trials as opportunities for growth: Understand that your trials and afflictions are temporary and serve as tests of your faith. As Christ and

His apostles have warned through the scriptures, you will face suffering and affliction. Embrace these challenges as opportunities to deepen your faith, knowing that you are never alone; God's strength and power are always accessible.

Cultivate a spiritual richness: Regardless of physical circumstances, remember that you are spiritually rich if you are in Christ. Just as Jesus reassured the church in Smyrna of their spiritual wealth amidst affliction and poverty, we, too, should focus on our spiritual resources. This involves regular engagement with scripture, prayer, and interaction with the local church, ensuring that our spiritual lives are robust and vibrant.

Live fearlessly in faith: Be inspired by the promise that Jesus gives to those who are faithful to the point of death— the crown of life. This assurance should motivate you to live fearlessly and commit fully to your faith, regardless of your trials. Practically, this means making decisions that align with God's will, even when they are counter-cultural or difficult.

Stay rooted in God's promises: Regularly remind yourself of God's promises and His unchanging character. Engage deeply with scriptures affirming God's commitment to His people and ultimate victory over evil, such as the promises in the book of Revelation. By doing so, you strengthen the foundation of your faith, ensuring that when storms come, your spiritual house stands firm.

Conclusion

Confidence is not just a helpful trait; it's necessary for a life rooted in faith. We need definitive answers with exclamation points, not the uncertainty of question marks. We don't wish for this certainty; we already possess it through God and His Word. Many wonder, "How do I know I'm going to heaven?" The answer lies in our commitment to following God's way to the best of our ability and our conviction that God's word is accurate. Based on these truths, you can know what is right and develop your faith.

This is especially important for young people who may question their path should their parents or mentors fall away or pass on. Would your faith endure without them? It's crucial to build confidence in the righteousness of our actions because they align with God's truth, not because they are validated by external approval from elders, preachers, parents, or friends.

Our commitment must build confidence in God and His way, underpinned by the unwavering truth that God cannot be wrong.

This unshakeable confidence fueled the Christians' perseverance and hope in Smyrna. They appeared to have nothing by worldly standards, but in God, they possessed everything, including eternal life. Their example shows us that having God's word deeply embedded in our hearts brings stability and certainty, rare commodities in a world where little else can be taken for granted. Have you placed your trust in Him? This question is fundamental, as your answer determines the strength and stability of your spiritual life. Trusting in God transforms your perspective, empowering you to face tough times with the assurance that, with God, you are indeed a possessor of eternal life.

For Reflection

1. What does it mean to have confidence in God, and how does this influence your daily decisions?

2. How can we cultivate steadfast faith even if influential figures, like parents or spiritual mentors, fall away or pass on?

3. Discuss a time when you experienced doubt. How did you regain confidence in your faith during that period?

4. What practical steps can you take to ensure your faith is based on God's word rather than seeking approval from others?

5. How does the assurance of eternal life influence your perspective on material possessions and worldly status?

6. In what ways does embedding God's word in your heart provide stability in your life?

7. Can you share an example from your life or someone you know where trust in God's plan provided peace in a difficult situation?

8. How does understanding that God cannot be wrong affect your response to life's uncertainties and challenges?

9. What role does personal Bible study play in building your confidence in God's promises?

10. How can the local church support its members in developing and maintaining a confident faith, especially among young people?

Lesson 10

The Experience and Wonder of Worship

An Encounter with God

Read: Luke 5:17–26; Isaiah 6:1–8.

Pray for help deepening your desire for worship and growing closer to God. Ask God to deepen your hunger for Him and give you an open mind and heart as you prepare to worship.

What is Worship?

When the word worship is mentioned, all sorts of definitions come to mind. Worship is "declaring the worth of God." In Old English, it was called *worthship*. Practically speaking, we don't worship God for what we get out of it. We worship to give God the honor due Him, to recognize His worth and value, and to acknowledge His place in and claim on our lives.

Before we go further, it is appropriate to discuss what worship is not:

- It is not a weekly pep talk to make us feel good about ourselves.
- It is not a rock concert or a symphony.
- It is not a motivational seminar.
- It is not an excursion into the acquisition of academic knowledge about scripture.

Worship occurs when people encounter the God who loves them and desires a relationship with them. It is a "meeting between God and His people." It does not *lead* to an encounter with God; *it is an encounter with God*. When we worship, we come with an agenda: *to meet with God*. When we worship, God has an agenda: *to meet with us*.

This should be considered each time we walk through the doors at our weekly service. When we do, it will impact us. It should affect our attitude, dress, and punctuality. It should also impact how we pay attention to what we're doing during the service. If you don't go to worship to meet God, you will not get anything out of the service.

The Realities of God's Presence

If worship is about encountering God's presence, someone might say: *I thought God's presence was always with us.* And indeed, He is, as explained in Psalm 139:8. God's omnipresence is a reality. We can't escape it. God is always there (Exodus 33:14; Matthew 18:20). Jesus' teaching in Matthew 18 indicates that God manifests His presence uniquely when we worship.

Before going further, we should consider Luke 5:17–26. Here, we observe an example of both God's omnipresence and His revealed presence. Jesus was there—that's omnipresence—He was in the middle of the crowd that heard Him come to preach. But notice the 2nd sentence in 5:17: *And the power of the Lord was with Him to heal.* What does Luke mean? This may not have been a physical manifestation of energy, but it was noticed. Jesus had the power to heal, and the Spirit gave it to Him. That power—that revealed presence—caused the people to glorify God after they witnessed the miracle.

> Then everyone was astounded, and they were giving glory to God. And they were filled with awe and said, "We have seen incredible things today" (Luke 5:26).

When you were with Jesus, you knew you were with God. You couldn't get enough. They were *astounded.* They *gave glory to God.* They were *filled with awe.* That's the extra glimpse of God we should crave. We should want to experience awe and amazement because we'll be forever changed when we do. We should ask for it.

What is Needed in Worship?

If you could ask God for anything, what would it be? Moses got the opportunity. He didn't ask for food, riches, or prestige. He desired something more profound, higher, and spiritual beyond this world—a hunger for God.

He asks, *please show me your ways … that I may know you,* (Exodus 33:13). Moses wanted to progressively become more deeply and intimately acquainted with God. He wanted to recognize more and understand clearly. He wasn't interested in God's ways just because he possessed information. He had the heart of a worshiper. He wanted to experience God every day in His life. He didn't just want the facts; He wanted God. He's talking about relationships.

Moses' Encounter with God

Moses asked, "Please, let me see your glory" (Exodus 33:18). Glory refers to "God's honor, renown, majesty, and His visible splendor." It is closely related to presence and face. Moses wanted to see God face to face. He wanted a visible encounter with God. He was not content with business as usual. He wanted God to show up in life. We need not only to hunger for God, but we need an encounter with God. We need a sense of His presence. When we get it, it will transform our worship from a:

- Duty to devotion.
- Ritual to relationship.
- A simple meeting to a holy gathering.

What Do We Need to Do?

Here are three life-changing actions we need to take to experience God's revealed presence in worship:

- **Anticipate God's presence.** Expect it. Long for it. Pray for it. Prepare yourself for it.
- **Look for His hand at work in worship.** Focus on the words used in our praise and prayer. How often do the words in a hymn or prayer directly apply to something you're dealing with in life? Do you chalk it up to luck or coincidence? How often has a word spoken by a shepherd, preacher, or teacher hit you squarely, and you know it is God speaking to you through His Word (Hebrews 4:12)?
- **Listen to God speaking to you through His word.** He has preserved scripture for a reason. Listen to the message. We're not just for gaining new information but to store up and invigorate your soul.

The Power of Worship

Our family last visited Yellowstone National Park in 2003 as a farewell tour before we moved back east to Indiana. We spent several days going around the park. As always, it is a unique and breathtaking experience. Where is the first place you want to visit if you've visited the park? *Old Faithful.* Why? It's not the tallest geyser or the most spectacular out of the hundreds in the park, but it is *faithful.* Every 35–120 minutes, hot water shoots straight up from the ground over a hundred feet for as little as 90 seconds or as long as 5 minutes. You can count on it. The National Park Service has even timed when the next eruption will occur.

When you're there, it's clearly the center of attention.

Tourists are everywhere. As the time approaches for the geyser to go off, the number of people grows as they crowd in on the boardwalk to watch. Everybody's phone is out—all pointed at a hole in the ground. At once, water starts sputtering. Then it stops. Then it starts again—water going 100 ft into the sky. Everyone is just amazed. Spellbound. Then, in a moment or two, it's over.

But the people's reaction is the same every time I go to Yellowstone. Hundreds of people are gathered on the boardwalk, moved in awe of having just experienced something powerful—something beyond themselves. When they leave there, they know they've experienced something spectacular.

A similar dynamic should occur when we worship God (This lesson is based off a series of sermons by Rick Ezell).

We should be able to see something spectacular—something beyond ourselves. We should leave filled with awe, mesmerized by God's life-giving, life-flowing power. We should be motivated to tell others about what we have experienced. What *Old Faithful* does for the tourist in Wyoming, our worship of God should do for us.

Psalm 40:3— Two Elements of Worship

He put a new song in my mouth, a hymn of praise to our God. Many will see and fear, and they will trust in the LORD (Psalm 40:3).

Here, we discover two profound elements: *celebration* and *proclamation*.

Celebration

He put a new song in my mouth, a hymn of praise to our God.

Think vertically. David had an experience with God. God had rescued and refreshed him. He had been in God's presence. He was changed. He couldn't keep silent about it. Notice how he is exuberant in his praise. He is excited. He can't contain his joy/happiness/relief. He *had* to shout for joy! It wasn't just any song he was singing—it was a *new* song, indicating a freshness or newness in his experience with God. It was as though he was seeing God again for the first time.

There hasn't been a time that I have visited Yellowstone National Park without visiting Old Faithful. You want to see it again and again. Every time you walk away, you are amazed and moved. That's the way it should be with worship. David's singing was not about him—it was about God. It was worship. It was an expression of gratitude to God for who He is, what He has said, and what He is doing. David knew that the source of everything he had was God himself.

Proclamation

Think horizontally.

Many will see and fear and put their trust in the Lord.

As David worshiped, many saw it. They saw him praising. They didn't just hear it. The security he gained and found in God—gave others the confidence to join and find it in worship. David's joy before God was a powerful testimony. It was inspirational. We don't just worship God at church. Worship should be a constant attitude and activity in our lives. At church, we worship publicly and corporately. And when we do, we proclaim the mightiness of our God. When people far from God hear those close to God moving with heartfelt praise, they are moved. It's like seeing *Old Faithful*. They're moved. They want to know how and why that happens.

Two Products of Worship

Spiritually Lost People Can Be Drawn to Jesus By Our Worship

It can be like a magnet.

> If, therefore, the whole church assembles together and all are speaking in tongues and people who are outsiders or unbelievers come in, will they not say that you are out of your minds? But if all are prophesying and some unbeliever or outsider comes in, he

> is convicted by all and is called to account by all. The secrets of his heart will be revealed, and as a result he will fall facedown and worship God, proclaiming, "God is really among you." What then, brothers and sisters? Whenever you come together, each one has a hymn, a teaching, a revelation, a tongue, or an interpretation. Everything is to be done for building up (1 Corinthians 14:23–26).

Here, Paul is amidst a discussion on the purpose of spiritual gifts. Tongues and prophecy are in view. Tongue speaking was speaking in a language other than one's own without a translator. Prophecy was the ability to reveal things directly from God as the scripture had not yet been completed.

Please focus on 14:24–25, where instructions are given for them to worship so that they know that unbelievers are in the assembly. Paul desired that the guest at worship would be *called to account by all, the secrets of his heart are disclosed, and so, falling on his face, he will worship God and declare that God is really among you*. What we do in the public worship service should be done with a consciousness that the unchurched may be present and how we conduct ourselves will influence them.

Now, let's look at John 12:32: *And I, when I am lifted up from the earth, will draw all people to myself.* Jesus is predicting His death…but the principle we're looking for here is that when Jesus is lifted up in praise and worship, lost people will be attracted to Him. Again, this is a product of worship, not the aim of worship. Worship is all about God, where we declare His worth.

Now, let's go back to the Old Testament:

> I will praise you, Lord, among the peoples; I will sing praises to you among the nations. For your faithful love is as high as the heavens; your faithfulness reaches the clouds. God, be exalted above the heavens; let your glory be over the whole earth (Psalm 57:9–11).

There is an evangelistic connection that arises from honest and heartfelt worship. When God's people experience His presence, they meet God and engage their hearts. Lives are changed and one of the results is that lost people can also be drawn into God's presence. The worldly person will take notice. Remember, the unchurched who come to our worship service are making judgments about God and us as they gather here. If they come in and see people unprepared, unengaged, uninterested, going through the motions, engaging in mere ritual, they'll leave and never come back.

But if our hearts are on fire, the lost will be drawn to Christ. We must never compromise the need to be prepared for worship. Worship leaders must be ready to lead in the Lord's Supper, giving, singing, and praying. *All of these are to be connected to the purpose of praise and adoration of God.* Not only do leaders need to move with this purpose—but all the participants.

The Scriptures teach that God draws people to Him through authentic worship by His people:

- Psalm 18:49: "Therefore I will thank you among the nations, LORD; I will praise your name."
- Romans 15:9: "and so that Gentiles may glorify God for his mercy. As it is written, Therefore I will praise you among the Gentiles, and I will sing praise to your name."
- Psalm 96:3: "Declare his glory among the nations, his wondrous works among all peoples."
- Psalm 138:4–5: "All the kings on earth will give you thanks, LORD, when they hear what you have promised. They will sing of the LORD's ways, for the LORD's glory is great."
- Psalm 145:10–12: "All you have made will thank you, LORD; the faithful will bless you. They will speak of the glory of your kingdom and will declare your might, informing all people of your mighty acts and of the glorious splendor of your kingdom."
- 2 Samuel 22:50: "Therefore I will give thanks to you among the nations, LORD; I will sing praises about your name."

More people are won to Christ by being moved by God's presence than by all the apologetic arguments combined. Few are converted to Jesus purely on intellectual grounds. Having a sense of God's presence melts hearts and explodes mental barriers. A seeker may not understand the meaning of a song or what happens in communion, but they know joy when they see it. They understand when lives are being impacted. They can read where lives are being changed. This will cause them to want what we have. If this is true, so is the opposite: *What happens when a seeker sees someone bored to tears, having a scowl on their face, incessantly yawning? Will they be attracted to Jesus?*

The Saved Are Sent Out to Share Jesus after Worship

Who hasn't been inspired to tell someone about Jesus after an inspirational worship service? *True worship affects believers.*

Isaiah 6:1–8 is a great example.

> In the year that King Uzziah died, I saw the Lord seated on a high and lofty throne, and the hem of his robe filled the temple. Seraphim were standing above him; they each had six wings: with two they covered their faces, with two they covered their feet, and with two they flew. And one called to another: Holy, holy, holy is the LORD of Armies; his glory fills the whole earth. The foundations of the doorways shook at the sound of their voices, and the temple was filled with smoke. Then I said: Woe is me for I am ruined because I am a man of unclean lips and live among a people of unclean lips, and because my eyes have seen the King, the LORD of Armies. Then one of the seraphim flew to me, and in his hand was a glowing coal that he had taken from the altar with tongs. He touched my mouth with it and said: Now that this has touched your lips, your iniquity is removed and your sin is atoned for. Then I heard the voice of the Lord asking: Who will I send? Who will go for us? I said: Here I am. Send me.

You are probably very familiar with verse 8: *Here I am! Send Me!* Please note that Isaiah was commissioned to speak for the people only after he saw and heard God. He would have missed God's calling if he had not entered worship.

In Matthew 28:16–20, Jesus gave the great commission. It is the reason for our spiritual existence. In it, we are charged to tell others about Jesus. Let's look at the context in which this command is given:

> The eleven disciples traveled to Galilee, to the mountain where Jesus had directed them. When they saw him, they worshiped, but some doubted (Matthew 28:16–17).

Focus on how the disciples saw Jesus and *they worshiped.* In this context, the command to share Jesus with the world is given inside the context of worship. From that (worship), they were called to go to all nations and represent Jesus. The same thing repeats itself in Acts 2:1–41 on the Day of Pentecost. The disciples were gathered for worship. It was the 50th day after the Passover. It's Sunday. *They're worshiping.* In verse 2, the Spirit descends. *What do they do?* They begin to declare *the mighty works of God* (2:11). Now, look at 2:38–41—what happens here? People saw and heard the message, experienced God, and responded in faith to the gospel call.

Evangelism springs from worship. Unbelievers are drawn to God through it, and their worship compels them to tell others about Him. Wholehearted worshipers call the whole world to wholehearted worship.

Two Challenges for Worshipers

What can you do? You can do what people do when they gather to watch *Old Faithful*. i.e., *find a place to meet God in worship.* Come to celebrate. Worship is a time to lay aside trouble, anxieties, and cares. Worship is a time to celebrate God's gift of mercy and grace and to experience God's forgiveness. It is a weekly opportunity to let God's power lift you out of the slimy pits of life and allow His provision to set you on firm footing. Every week, you get to proclaim a *new song* by lifting hymns of praise to God. You can tell others about your experience. We don't just do this for ourselves. We invite others to join with us. We call on others to come into God's presence and stand before the throne, to come to the mountaintop.

What's In This for Us?

Anticipate and prepare for encounter: Approach worship with the anticipation of meeting God. Just as we prepare for important meetings or events, we should prepare spiritually and mentally for encountering God's presence. This means coming with an open heart and mind, ready to engage in worship rather than passively attending.

Engage actively: Worship is not a spectator sport but an active engagement with God. Pay attention to the words of songs, prayers, and teachings, seeking to connect them with your own life experiences and spiritual growth. Actively participate in worship rather than simply going through the motions.

Seek God's presence daily: Like Moses, cultivate a hunger for God's presence in your daily life, not just during designated corporate worship times. Seek to know God more deeply and intimately, desiring to experience Him in every aspect of your life. This involves prioritizing spiritual disciplines such as prayer, meditation on scripture, and fellowship with your spiritual family.

Reflect God's glory: As worshipers, our lives should reflect God's glory to those around us. Just as David's joyful worship attracted others to God, our genuine worship should inspire curiosity and draw others to seek God. Let your worship testify to God's transforming power in your life, inviting others to experience His presence for themselves.

Conclusion

While God does not need your worship, He delights in it. Are you telling others about Christ? Are you inviting others into God's presence? You can be drawn to Him. You are to worship. But God doesn't want you to stay there. He wants to send you out and have you testify about Him. It's like seeing *Old Faithful*, basking in its glory and splendor, but you must go home. You don't live on the boardwalk around the geyser. But once you've seen it, you must tell others about it.

For Reflection

1. How does our understanding of worship as "declaring the worth of God" shape our approach to Sunday services and daily life?

2. How do the misconceptions of worship mentioned in the lesson (e.g., weekly pep talk, rock concert) affect our personal worship experiences?

3. Reflecting on Moses' desire to see God's glory, how can we cultivate a similar hunger for encountering God in our lives?

4. How does the concept of God's omnipresence challenge or reinforce our understanding of worship as encountering His unique presence?

5. Discuss authentic worship's impact on believers and non-believers, as illustrated in the lesson through examples like David's praise and Isaiah's commission.

6. What practical steps can we take to actively engage in worship rather than passively participating?

7. How can we ensure that our worship is not just a ritual or duty but a genuine expression of devotion and relationship with God?

8. Reflect on the idea that worship should transform our lives from a simple meeting to a holy gathering. How does this transformation manifest in our attitudes, actions, and interactions with others?

9. Consider the connection between worship and evangelism. How does our worship influence those around us, both believers and non-believers?

10. How can we encourage one another to prioritize and pursue authentic worship experiences that lead to encountering God's presence in our lives?

Lesson 11

The Excitement of Sharing Our Hope

The Natural Expression of the Life of a Christian

Read: Titus 2:5–10; 3:1–8.

Pray for help sharing the gospel and for God to find someone you can talk to about Him. Pray for courage and the right words. Pray for help leading the kind of life that will attractively demonstrate the life-changing power of the gospel.

Introduction

Now that you're in God's family, you have been given a tremendous opportunity to share the gospel with others you meet. These might be your spouse, children, parents, and extended family. There are friends in your life who are outside Christ. You may have business acquaintances or people at work who need to hear the good news. Potential prospects are everywhere!

Sharing Jesus is not a program sponsored by the local congregation. It is the natural expression of the life of a Christian. We have been given hope through the gift of salvation—now, our transformed heart yearns to share what we have with others. God's plan for sharing the gospel is not complicated. It simply comes down to each person talking to one other person who talks to one other person, and the growth begins to take on exponential proportions. And it's all driven by personal, warm relationships we build over time with lost people. They witness the impact of our transformation, see how we make our lives around something eternal, and are moved by how we handle the challenges life presents. Your hope, joy, and rock-solid perseverance through life's circumstances is a fantastic testimony for Jesus.

Every Christian can do this. *You can do this.* As you reflect on your own spiritual adoption story, you can describe the incredible delivering power of Jesus. You can talk about where things were headed in your life, where they are now, and *who* is responsible. You can reassure others that as you've gone through life, there was One who got you through by His sustaining power. There are no lines you have to remember. There are no sets of bullet points. It's just you being relatable about what you know best—your adoption story filled with hope, amazement, and joy. This makes the gospel attractive in any era, especially our own, as we see many people hurting and looking for lasting hope.

In this lesson, we'll look at Titus' mission as he ministered on the island of Crete. He had a very challenging situation. Paul described the Cretans as rebellious, *full of empty talk and deception* (Titus 1:10). He even cited one of their own who described them as *liars, evil beasts, and lazy gluttons* (Titus 1:12). Can you imagine going into this type of place trying to preach or plant a church? The societal conditions in Crete were similar to the entire Greco-Roman world. The call of Christianity was the ultimate in what it means to be counter-cultural. Remember, Christians were operating without a Bible, no underlying cultural influence of Christian morality, and hardly any voices loud enough to sway a world empire. Paganism and all its allures were the mainstream.

So, how did the early church respond?

How they responded is how we must respond in our own time, i.e., reaching one unsaved person at a time with the power of the gospel. For them, there was no other agenda.

Titus' Mission is Our Mission

Titus' mission was to get the gospel into the public so people could hear it. The most effective way that could be carried out was demonstrating redemption through redeemed lives. The entire thrust of Paul's letter to Titus is the need to convert the lost. The theme of the book is salvation. Paul emphasizes:

- God is our Savior (1:3; 2:10; 3:4).
- Jesus is our Savior (1:4; 2:13; 3:6).
- The Spirit performs the action of salvation in baptism (3:5b–6).

This is the message. As we deliver the message, what must we keep in mind? We must live and conduct ourselves in a way that:

- God's word will not be slandered (2:5).
- Our opponents will have nothing bad to say about us (2:8).
- We adorn the teaching of God our Savior in everything (2:10).

The mission is to get the gospel into the public's ears. We do this primarily by demonstrating redemption through our redeemed lives. Everything we do in life becomes an opportunity to share Jesus and discuss how He directs our new life.

Three Things We Need to Remember About Our Mission

If we are going to be successful in sharing the gospel, we must keep three essential things in mind:

Remember Your Responsibility to Society

In our age of self-expression, independence, and selfishness, we may not concentrate on these virtues as we should. Check out Titus 3:1–2:

> Remind them to submit to rulers and authorities, obey, be ready for every good work, slander no one, avoid fighting, and be kind, always showing gentleness to all people.

Let's talk about each of the things Paul lists:

- Be submissive to rulers and authorities. We may not always agree, but we pray for them and follow their lead when they do what is right.
- Be obedient. (A parallel passage is found in 2 Timothy 2:21, where we are called vessels of honor ready for every good work.)
- Ready for every good work.
- Slander no one, i.e., *speak evil of no one.*
- Avoid fighting, i.e., *quarreling.*
- Be kind.
- Show gentleness to all people.

These are fundamental principles of citizenship—good behavior in everyday life. Christians should not be known for being contentious, fighting, or protesting. We trust in God to make things right when we suffer wrong. Why is this so important? The world is watching now more than ever. How are you responding during times of crisis? What do others see in your social media feeds?

Remember Your Former Condition

> For we too were once foolish, disobedient, deceived, enslaved by various passions and pleasures, living in malice and envy, hateful, detesting one another (Titus 3:3).

Before we attack the world with its problems and view ourselves as a cultural warrior, we need to remember who we once were. The contrast is between our former status (dead) vs. our present regenerated condition.

We were:

- Rebellious to God's law.
- Resistant to His truth.
- Open to mindless passion.
- Fed on the bad treatment of others.

These types of passive and active things characterize the rest of humanity. What Paul describes here once described us, which should humble us all.

Remember Your Salvation

> But when the kindness of God our Savior and his love for mankind appeared, he saved us—not by works of righteousness that we had done, but according to his mercy—through the washing of regeneration and renewal by the Holy Spirit. He poured out his Spirit on us abundantly through Jesus Christ our Savior so that, having been justified by his grace, we may become heirs with the hope of eternal life (Titus 3:4–7).

God has saved you. Jesus is the basis of your salvation. Your salvation wasn't by your work. It was by the mercy of God. What makes this even more impressive is that God took the initiative to save us while we were still aligned against Him, i.e., an enemy (Romans 5:8–10). God saved us when we surrendered our will to Him in baptism. Before that, we were wretched and hopelessly lost. It was God who renewed you by the Holy Spirit. Think of how this strikes the heart of human pride. There is no reason ever to exalt ourselves. The emphasis is on God. His grace, power, mercy, and activity in saving us are all in complete focus.

This will change how we look at the world. Evangelism will become a natural expression of a humble, saved heart that trusts God. We've all been inside the pit. Thank God He pulled us out. Let's tell everyone that He can do the same for them.

What's In This for Us?

Authenticity in evangelism: Sharing Jesus isn't a scripted program but a natural expression of a changed life. In modern times, where authenticity is valued, our personal stories of transformation can resonate deeply with others. We can share the hope and joy we've found in Christ through genuine, warm relationships built over time.

Cultural relevance: Just as Titus faced a challenging cultural backdrop, we encounter diverse societal norms and values today. Our mission remains counter-cultural, emphasizing redemption through transformed lives. In today's world filled with distractions and competing ideologies, our commitment to living out the gospel becomes a powerful testimony that draws others to Christ.

Principles of citizenship: Our responsibility to society extends beyond the walls of our churches. We're called to embody daily virtues such as submission, obedience, kindness, and gentleness. In an age marked by division and conflict, our conduct as Christians speaks volumes about our faith. By upholding these principles, we demonstrate the gospel's power in action.

Humility and gratitude: Reflecting on our former condition reminds us of God's grace and mercy. We were once lost and hopeless, but God intervened and saved us through His kindness and love. This humbling realization should fuel our evangelistic efforts, prompting us to share the hope of salvation with others. Our salvation story becomes a powerful tool for reaching those hurting and searching for lasting hope in a world of uncertainty.

Conclusion

> This saying is trustworthy. I want you to insist on these things so that those who believe in God might be careful to devote themselves to good works. These are good and profitable for everyone (Titus 3:8).

What we've explored in this lesson is a firm foundation of truth. As someone our heavenly Father has adopted, we can confidently proclaim the gospel, knowing its power remains unchanged.

Let us continually uphold the three foundational principles: living in a manner that honors God's word, speaking in a manner that reflects Christ's character, and adorning the doctrine of Christ through our actions. May we always remember our responsibility to society, our former condition before salvation, and the miraculous gift of our salvation. In doing so, we embody the powerful message of the gospel and invite others to experience the same hope and redemption we've found in Jesus Christ.

For Reflection

1. How does the unchanging power of the gospel inspire your confidence in sharing your faith with others?

2. How can you actively live out the foundational principles of honoring God's word, reflecting Christ's character, and adorning Christ's doctrine daily?

3. Reflecting on your transformation, how has remembering your former condition before salvation impacted your understanding of God's grace and mercy?

4. What steps can you take as a Christian to fulfill your responsibility to society, especially in today's cultural context?

5. Consider a time when someone's changed life or testimony profoundly impacted you. How did it influence your perception of Christianity?

6. How does the gift of salvation motivate you to share the gospel with others, searching for hope and redemption?

7. How can you ensure that your words and actions consistently reflect the character of Christ, especially when faced with challenges or opposition?

8. Reflect on a specific instance in which you experienced the power of the gospel in your life. How does that experience help your approach to evangelism?

9. What practical steps can you take to maintain a humble attitude as you share the gospel, recognizing that salvation is a gift from God?

10. How does the timeless truth of the gospel encourage you to persevere in sharing your faith, even with changing cultural norms and societal pressures?

Lesson 12

A Wealth of Spiritual Blessings

Embracing our Identity and Inheritance in Christ

Before You Begin

Read: Ephesians 1:3–14.

Pray for a greater understanding of what it means to grasp your identity in Christ and the richness of the blessings you have received in Christ. Also, pray that as you grow in understanding these things, your words and interactions with others will bring glory to God.

Introduction

Ephesians is Paul's letter that stresses the theology of the church, which is the body of Christ (1:22). As part of His church, we find reconciliation with God and one another (2:16), become an heir of the promise (3:6), and become a member of *His body* (5:30), with Jesus as the head (1:22–23). What I've just written should not be seen as a mere collection of facts or mundane doctrinal teaching. *It means something. As an adopted son or daughter of God,* He called you through the gospel to be a part of this wondrous body. It is a special thing to be a part of God's church.

Ultimately, God created you and saved you for His glory.

> We know that all things work together for the good of those who love God, who are called according to his purpose. For those he foreknew he also predestined to be conformed to the image of his Son, so that he would be the firstborn among many brothers and sisters. And those he predestined, he also called; and those he called, he also justified; and those he justified, he also glorified (Romans 8:28–30).

Do you see the result of what happened when you responded to His call? You were *justified*. You were and are in the process of being *sanctified*. And ultimately, God is aiming for your *glorification*. You have been created for His glory. You mean something. You are important to Him.

As part of His church, you are part of something that began in eternity past. Before the world began, God designed the church so we could be together with Him for eternity. The faithful—those who are part of Christ's body, the church, are part of God's great, all-embracing, eternal purpose:

> For he chose us in him, before the foundation of the world, to be holy and blameless in love before him (Ephesians 1:4).

Paul's choice in verse 4 reveals God's character, plan, and action in redeeming people. The fact that you have been saved reveals the result of God's initiative. Your salvation is not an accident or an afterthought:

- It was according to *His will* (1:5).
- It was according to *grace* (1:6–7).
- It was according to *His purpose* (1:11).

Why is this so important?

We need to see ourselves in God's plan and understand our extreme value to God and the richness of our blessings. Today, many people are concerned about their self-worth. They search for a sense of value or self-acceptance. They want to be someone who matters. Perhaps this is why we've all become so addicted to social media. We want an identity. Today, we have self-help books that teach you how to be successful, get on top, and believe in yourself. Some are concerned about their ancestry and view everything through that lens. Maybe some of this is just a way for people to give themselves meaning when they're not sure what their meaning is. Some try to establish their identity in their righteousness. To keep themselves going, they constantly work to draw attention to what they're doing, how they're right, etc. You don't have to do all these things to find self-worth. You can discover a sense of significance, happiness, and joy by understanding who you are in Christ. And if you're looking for an identity—*this is the one that matters*.

Your value comes because you are in Christ. Realizing you are part of a group of people chosen in Christ before the world's foundation revolutionizes your life.

Ephesians 1:3– Praise for Spiritual Blessings

After a short introduction, Paul begins the letter to the Ephesians by praising our God, the essence of all that is good. Ours is the God who loves to give. We've already read from Romans 8:28, which speaks of His work and involvement in our lives. James said every good and perfect gift is from above, coming down from the father of lights, who does not change like shifting shadows (James 1:17). God is all about good and loves to shower blessings on His children. He has so blessed you that you are rich in Christ. You have been blessed beyond imagination.

How Have You Been Blessed?

Ephesians 1:3 says God has blessed us with every spiritual blessing in the heavens in Christ. You have every spiritual resource at your disposal. Just look at what Paul details in Ephesians:

- 1:3—We are blessed with every spiritual blessing.
- 1:4—We have been predestined to be adopted as sons.
- 1:7—We have redemption.
- 1:7—We have forgiveness.
- 1:8—We have wisdom.
- 1:11—We have an inheritance (spiritual wealth).
- 1:13—We have security, having been sealed with the Spirit.
- 1:18—We have hope.
- 1:18—We have an inheritance and immense spiritual wealth.
- 1:19—We have power.
- 2:4-6—We are alive with new life.
- 2:7—We are objects of eternal grace.
- 2:10—We are God's masterpiece.
- 2:10—We are called to a life of good works.
- 2:13-18—We are one with God and every other Christian.
- 2:19—We are members of God's family.
- 2:22—We are the habitation of the Spirit.
- 3:20—We are powerful beyond our imagination.
- 3:21—We can bring glory to God.
- 4:3—We possess the Spirit of God in us.
- 4:4-6—We are members of the body of Christ.
- 4:11-13—We have received gifts/talents and gifted men who lead us to maturity for ministry work.
- 4:20-24—We have Jesus who teaches us the new walk of life.
- 5:1-2—We have the love of God, which teaches us how to walk in love.

- 5:8—We have received light so that we may dwell in light.
- 5:14–17—We have received wisdom & truth so that we may walk wisely in the world.
- 5:18—We have received the power of the fullness of the Spirit of God.
- 5:21—6.9—We have received every resource to make every human relationship what God intended.
- 6:10–17—We have received invulnerable, invincible, fantastic, powerful armor against which Satan can't stand… if we use it.
- 6:16—We have the sword of the Spirit, the Word of God, which is in the hand of every believer.

Do We Realize God Has Already Dispensed with Every Spiritual Blessing?

We may be spending much time asking for what we've already got. What does Peter say?

> His divine power **has given us** everything required for life and godliness through the knowledge of him who called us by his own glory and goodness (1 Peter 1:3).

You have every resource to get through this life to the next.

Look at Ephesians 1:17. Since this is true…, and since having every spiritual blessing is our present reality, *what should we be praying for?*

> I pray that the God of our Lord Jesus Christ, the glorious Father, would give you the Spirit of wisdom and revelation in the knowledge of him.

We need to be praying for a greater ability to realize the blessings we have already received.

Where Are Our Blessings?

The divine realm. They are *in the heavens.* The challenge is for us to elevate our perspective to see them. Heaven is home. God is there. Jesus is there. All the Bible heroes are there. Our loved ones are there. We live in two worlds—but only one of them is home. We may have nothing in this world, but in the one to come, we're so rich that it's unimaginable.

Now, the question is, how do we realize our blessings here on earth? We do so when we *walk by the Spirit* (Galatians 5:16–24). When we do this, we experience love, joy, peace, patience, kindness, goodness, faithfulness, gentleness, and self-control.

Our Blessings are *In Christ*

All that is His is yours. We have all the resources He has. *We are as rich as He is.*

> The Spirit himself testifies together with our spirit that we are God's children, and if children, also heirs—heirs of God and co-heirs with Christ—if indeed we suffer with him so that we may also be glorified with him (Romans 8:16–17).

You are part of the church planned from before the world began. You are a joint heir with Christ. By walking by the Spirit—it all becomes yours. **That's rich.** No wonder Paul praised God. It's a marvelous reality. You are in Christ, so:

- His position is your position.
- His privilege is your privilege.
- His possession is your possession.
- And His practice is your practice.

Where He is, I am. What He has, I have. And what He does, I do.

What's In This for Us?

What an incredible feeling! God has eternally formed His body. As a Christian, you are part of that. If you're struggling with self-worth, *you are worthy.* If you're fighting feelings of inadequacy, *God has poured out every spiritual blessing in the heavens over you.* The resources available to you are unlimited.

> Now to him who is able to do above and beyond all that we ask or think according to the power that works in us (Ephesians 3:20).

You need to use the blessings.

You need to capitalize on them to live the life God intends for you.

Conclusion

Paul not only celebrates the abundant spiritual blessings we possess in Christ—ranging from wisdom and redemption to power and divine armor—but also our intrinsic worth and purpose in God's eternal plan. We are not just recipients of God's blessings; we are active participants in His divine story, chosen before the world's creation to lead lives of holiness and love.

As we recognize and embrace our position in Christ, we are called to live out this identity practically through the Spirit's power, which enables us to manifest the fruits of love, joy, peace, and self-control. By walking in the Spirit, we actualize the blessings already bestowed upon us in the heavens, making them a reality in our daily lives. Therefore, the challenge and invitation for us is to elevate our perspective, live out our God-given identity, and engage fully with the resources we have been given to glorify God and enrich our brothers and sisters in Christ. Through this, we find our value and meaning and contribute to unfolding God's glorious purpose on earth.

For Reflection

1. How does understanding our identity as members of Christ's body change how we interact with other believers and non-believers?

2. How can we practically "walk by the Spirit" to experience and manifest the fruits of the Spirit in our daily lives?

3. Discuss the concept of being chosen by God before the foundation of the world. How does this knowledge impact our sense of self-worth and purpose?

4. Ephesians mentions that we are blessed with every spiritual blessing in the heavenly realms. Can you share a personal experience where you felt you accessed these blessings?

5. How can the realization that we are co-heirs with Christ influence our attitudes toward suffering and challenges in life?

6. What does it mean to be God's masterpiece, created for good works, as mentioned in Ephesians 2:10? How does this shape our understanding of our church and world roles?

7. Ephesians 1:17 speaks of the "Spirit of wisdom and revelation" in knowing God more. How can we actively seek this more profound knowledge and connection with God?

8. Considering that our real blessings and riches are in the heavenly realms, how should this truth affect our values and priorities in the material world?

9. Discuss the implications of being "sealed with the Holy Spirit" (Ephesians 1:13). How does this assurance affect our security and confidence as believers?

10. Reflect on the phrase "His divine power has given us everything we need for life and godliness" from 2 Peter 1:3. How does this statement encourage you in both spiritual and practical aspects?

www.ingramcontent.com/pod-product-compliance
Lightning Source LLC
Chambersburg PA
CBHW040322050426

42453CB00017B/2431